BERTRAND RUSSELL

THE CONQUEST OF HAPPINESS

Russell.

LONDON · UNWIN BOOKS

First Published in 1930
Second Impression 1930
Third Impression 1930
Fourth Impression 1931
Fifth Impression 1932
Sixth Impression 1937
Seventh Impression 1942
Eighth Impression 1944
Ninth Impression 1945
Tenth Impression 1948
Eleventh Impression 1951
Twelfth Impression 1956
First published in this Edition 1961
Second Impression 1962
Third Impression 1962
Fourth Impression 1963
Fifth Impression 1965
Sixth Impression 1967
Seventh Impression 1970
Eighth Impression 1971

ISBN: 0 04 171003 7

UNWIN BOOKS
*George Allen & Unwin Ltd
Ruskin House, Museum Street
London W.C.1*

PRINTED IN GREAT BRITAIN BY
LOWE AND BRYDONE (PRINTERS) LTD., LONDON

PREFACE

THIS book is not addressed to the learned, or to those who regard a practical problem merely as something to be talked about. No profound philosophy or deep erudition will be found in the following pages. I have aimed only at putting together some remarks which are inspired by what I hope is common sense. All that I claim for the recipes offered to the reader is that they are such as are confirmed by my own experience and observation, and that they have increased my own happiness whenever I have acted in accordance with them. On this ground I venture to hope that some among those multitudes of men and women who suffer unhappiness without enjoying it, may find their situation diagnosed and a method of escape suggested. It is in the belief that many people who are unhappy could become happy by well-directed effort that I have written this book.

I THINK I could turn and live with animals, they are so placid
and self-contained,
I stand and look at them long and long.
They do not sweat and whine about their condition,
They do not lie awake in the dark and weep for their sins,
They do not make me sick discussing their duty to God,
Not one is dissatisfied, not one is demented with the mania of
owning things,
Not one kneels to another, nor to his kind that lived thousands
of years ago,
Not one is respectable or unhappy over the whole earth.

WALT WHITMAN

CONTENTS

PART I
CAUSES OF UNHAPPINESS

CHAPTER I

What Makes People Unhappy?

ANIMALS are happy so long as they have health and enough to eat. Human beings, one feels, ought to be, but in the modern world they are not, at least in a great majority of cases. If you are unhappy yourself, you will probably be prepared to admit that you are not exceptional in this. If you are happy, ask yourself how many of your friends are so. And when you have reviewed your friends, teach yourself the art of reading faces; make yourself receptive to the moods of those whom you meet in the course of an ordinary day.

> A mark in every face I meet,
> Marks of weakness, marks of woe

says Blake. Though the kinds are different, you will find that unhappiness meets you everywhere. Let us suppose that you are in New York, the most typically modern of great cities. Stand in a busy street during working hours, or on a main thoroughfare at a week-end, or at a dance of an evening; empty your mind of your own ego, and let the personalities of the strangers about you take possession of you one after another. You will find that each of these different crowds has its own trouble. In the work-hour crowd you will see anxiety, excessive concentration, dyspepsia, lack of interest in anything but the struggle, incapacity for play, unconsciousness of their fellow creatures. On a main road at the week-end you will see men and women, all comfortably off, and some very rich, engaged in the pursuit of pleasure. This pursuit is conducted by all at a uniform pace, that of the slowest car in the procession; it is impossible to see the road for the cars, or the scenery since looking aside would cause an accident; all the occupants of all the cars are absorbed in the desire to pass other cars, which they cannot do on account of the crowd; if their minds wander from this preoccupation, as will happen occasionally to

those who are not themselves driving, unutterable boredom seizes
upon them and stamps their features with trivial discontent. Once
in a way a car-load of coloured people will show genuine enjoyment, but will cause indignation by erratic behaviour, and
ultimately get into the hands of the police owing to an accident:
enjoyment in holiday time is illegal.

Or, again, watch people at a gay evening. All come determined
to be happy, with the kind of grim resolve with which one deter-
mines not to make a fuss at the dentist's. It is held that drink and
petting are the gateways to joy, so people get drunk quickly, and
try not to notice how much their partners disgust them. After a
sufficient amount of drink, men begin to weep, and to lament how
unworthy they are, morally, of the devotion of their mothers. All
that alcohol does for them is to liberate the sense of sin, which
reason suppresses in saner moments.

The causes of these various kinds of unhappiness lie partly in the
social system, partly in individual psychology—which, of course, is
itself to a considerable extent a product of the social system. I have
written before about the changes in the social system required to
promote happiness. Concerning the abolition of war, of economic
exploitation, of education in cruelty and fear, it is not my intention
to speak in this volume. To discover a system for the avoidance of
war is a vital need for our civilization; but no such system has a
chance while men are so unhappy that mutual extermination seems
to them less dreadful than continued endurance of the light of day.
To prevent the perpetuation of poverty is necessary if the benefits
of machine production are to accrue in any degree to those most in
need of them; but what is the use of making everybody rich if the
rich themselves are miserable? Education in cruelty and fear is
bad, but no other kind can be given by those who are themselves
the slaves of these passions. These considerations lead us to the
problem of the individual: what can a man or woman, here and
now, in the midst of our nostalgic society, do to achieve happiness
for himself or herself? In discussing this problem, I shall confine
my attention to those who are not subject to any extreme cause of
outward misery. I shall assume a sufficient income to secure food
and shelter, sufficient health to make ordinary bodily activities
possible. I shall not consider the great catastrophes, such as loss of

all one's children, or public disgrace. There are things to be said about such matters, and they are important things, but they belong to a different order from the things that I wish to say. My purpose is to suggest a cure for the ordinary day-to-day unhappiness from which most people in civilized countries suffer, and which is all the more unbearable because, having no obvious external cause, it appears inescapable. I believe this unhappiness to be very largely due to mistaken views of the world, mistaken ethics, mistaken habits of life, leading to destruction of that natural zest and appetite for possible things upon which all happiness, whether of men or animals, ultimately depends. These are matters which lie within the power of the individual, and I propose to suggest the changes by which his happiness, given average good fortune, may be achieved.

Perhaps the best introduction to the philosophy which I wish to advocate will be a few words of autobiography. I was not born happy. As a child, my favourite hymn was: 'Weary of earth and laden with my sin.' At the age of five, I reflected that, if I should live to be seventy, I had only endured, so far, a fourteenth part of my whole life, and I felt the long-spread-out boredom ahead of me to be almost unendurable. In adolescence, I hated life and was continually on the verge of suicide, from which, however, I was restrained by the desire to know more mathematics. Now, on the contrary, I enjoy life; I might almost say that with every year that passes I enjoy it more. This is due partly to having discovered what were the things that I most desired and having gradually acquired many of these things. Partly it is due to having success-fully dismissed certain objects of desire—such as the acquisition of indubitable knowledge about something or other—as essentially unattainable. But very largely it is due to a diminishing pre-occupation with myself. Like others who had a Puritan education, I had the habit of meditating on my sins, follies, and shortcomings. I seemed to myself—no doubt justly—a miserable specimen. Gradually I learned to be indifferent to myself and my deficiencies; I came to centre my attention increasingly upon external objects: the state of the world, various branches of knowledge, individuals for whom I felt affection. External interests, it is true, bring each its own possibility of pain: the world may be plunged in war, knowledge in some direction may be hard to achieve, friends may die. But pains of these kinds do not destroy the essential quality of life, as do those that spring from disgust with self. And every external interest inspires some activity which, so long as the interest remains alive, is a complete preventive of *ennui*. Interest in oneself, on the contrary, leads to no activity of a progressive kind. It may lead to the keeping of a diary, to getting psycho-analysed, or perhaps to becoming a monk. But the monk will not be happy until the routine of the monastery has made him forget his own soul. The happiness which he attributes to religion he could have obtained from becoming a crossing-sweeper, provided he were compelled to remain one. External discipline is the only road to happiness for those unfortunates whose self-absorption is too profound to be cured in any other way.

Self-absorption is of various kinds. We may take the sinner, the narcissist, and the megalomaniac as three very common types.

When I speak of 'the sinner', I do not mean the man who commits sins: sins are committed by everyone or no one, according to our definition of the word. I mean the man who is absorbed in the consciousness of sin. This man is perpetually incurring his own disapproval, which, if he is religious, he interprets as the disapproval of God. He has an image of himself as he thinks he ought to be, which is in continual conflict with his knowledge of himself as he is. If, in his conscious thought, he has long since discarded the maxims that he was taught at his mother's knee, his sense of sin may be buried deep in his unconscious, and only emerge when he is drunk or asleep. Nevertheless, it may suffice to take the savour out of everything. At bottom he still accepts all the prohibitions he was taught in infancy. Swearing is wicked; drinking is wicked; ordinary business shrewdness is wicked; above all, sex is wicked. He does not, of course, abstain from any of these pleasures, but they are all poisoned for him by the feeling that they degrade him. The one pleasure that he desires with his whole soul is that of being approvingly caressed by his mother, which he can remember having experienced in childhood. This pleasure being no longer open to him, he feels that nothing matters: since he *must* sin, he decides to sin deeply. When he falls in love he looks for maternal tenderness, but cannot accept it, because, owing to the mother-image, he feels no respect for any woman with whom he has sexual relations. Then, in his disappointment, he becomes cruel, repents of his cruelty, and starts afresh on the dreary round of imagined sin and real remorse. This is the psychology of very many apparently hard-boiled reprobates. What drives them astray is devotion to an unattainable object (mother or mother-substitute) together with the inculcation, in early years, of a ridiculous ethical code. Liberation from the tyranny of early beliefs and affections is the first step towards happiness for these victims of maternal 'virtue'.

Narcissism is, in a sense, the converse of an habitual sense of sin; it consists in the habit of admiring oneself and wishing to be admired. Up to a point it is, of course, normal, and not to be deplored; it is only in its excesses that it becomes a grave evil. In many women, especially rich Society women, the capacity for feeling love is completely dried up, and is replaced by a powerful desire that all men should love them. When a woman of this kind is sure that a man loves her, she has no further use for him. The same thing occurs, though less frequently, with men; the classic example is the hero of *Liaisons Dangereuses*. When vanity is carried to this height, there is no genuine interest in any other person, and therefore no real satisfaction to be obtained from love. Other interests fail even more disastrously. A narcissist, for example, inspired by the homage paid to great painters, may become an art student; but, as painting is for him a mere means to an end, the technique never becomes interesting, and no subject can be seen except in relation to self. The result is failure and disappointment, with ridicule instead of the expected adulation. The same thing applies to those novelists whose novels always have themselves idealized as heroines. All serious success in work depends upon some genuine interest in the material with which the work is concerned. The tragedy of one successful politician after another is the gradual substitution of narcissism for an interest in the community and the measures for which he stands. The man who is only interested in himself is not admirable, and is not felt to be so. Consequently the man whose sole concern with the world is that it shall admire him is not likely to achieve his object. But even if he does, he will not be completely happy, since human instinct is never completely self-centred, and the narcissist is limiting himself artificially just as truly as is the man dominated by a sense of sin. The primitive man might be proud of being a good hunter, but he also enjoyed the activity of the chase. Vanity, when it passes beyond a point, kills pleasure in every activity for its own sake, and thus leads inevitably to listlessness and boredom. Often its source is diffidence, and its cure lies in the growth of self-respect. But this is only to be gained by successful activity inspired by objective interests.

The megalomaniac differs from the narcissist by the fact that he wishes to be powerful rather than charming, and seeks to be feared rather than loved. To this type belong many lunatics and most of the great men in history. Love of power, like vanity, is a strong element in normal human nature, and as such is to be accepted; it becomes deplorable only when it is excessive or associated with an insufficient sense of reality. Where this occurs it makes a man unhappy or foolish if not both. The lunatic who thinks he is a crowned head may be, in a sense, happy, but his happiness is not of a kind that any sane person would envy. Alexander the Great was psychologically of the same type as the lunatic, though he possessed the talent to achieve the lunatic's dream. He could not, however, achieve his own dream, which enlarged its scope as his achievement grew. When it became clear that he was the greatest conqueror known to fame, he decided that he was a God. Was he a happy man? His drunkenness, his furious rages, his indifference to women, and his claim to divinity, suggest that he was not. There is no ultimate satisfaction in the cultivation of one element of human nature at the expense of all the others, nor in viewing all the world as raw material for the magnificence of one's own ego. Usually the megalomaniac, whether insane or nominally sane, is the product of some excessive humiliation. Napoleon suffered at school from inferiority to his schoolfellows, who were rich aristocrats, while he was a penurious scholarship boy. When he allowed the return of the *émigrés*, he had the satisfaction of seeing his former schoolfellows bowing down before him. What bliss! Yet it led to the wish to obtain a similar satisfaction at the expense of the Czar, and this led to Saint Helena. Since no man can be omnipotent, a life dominated wholly by love of power can hardly fail, sooner or later, to meet with obstacles that cannot be overcome. The knowledge that this is so can only be prevented from obtruding on consciousness by some form of lunacy, though if a man is sufficiently great he can imprison or execute those who point this out to him. Repressions in the political and in the psycho-analytic senses thus go hand in hand. And wherever psycho-analytic repression in any marked form takes place, there is no genuine happiness. Power kept within its proper bounds may add greatly to happiness, but as the sole end of life it leads to disaster, inwardly if not outwardly.

The psychological causes of unhappiness, it is clear, are many and various. But all have something in common. The typical unhappy man is one who, having been deprived in youth of some normal satisfaction, has come to value this one kind of satisfaction more than any other, and has therefore given to his life a one-sided direction, together with a quite undue emphasis upon the achievement as opposed to the activities connected with it. There is, however, a further development which is very common in the present day. A man may feel so completely thwarted that he seeks no form of satisfaction, but only distraction and oblivion. He then becomes a devotee of 'pleasure'. That is to say he seeks to make life bearable by becoming less alive. Drunkenness, for example, is temporary suicide; the happiness that it brings is merely negative, a momentary cessation of unhappiness. The narcissist and the megalomaniac believe that happiness is possible, though they may adopt mistaken means of achieving it; but the man who seeks intoxication, in whatever form, has given up hope except in oblivion. In his case, the first thing to be done is to persuade him that happiness is desirable. Men who are unhappy, like men who sleep badly, are always proud of the fact. Perhaps their pride is like that of the fox who had lost his tail; if so, the way to cure it is to point out to them how they can grow a new tail. Very few men, I believe, will deliberately choose unhappiness if they see a way of being happy. I do not deny that such men exist, but they are not sufficiently numerous to be important. I shall therefore assume that the reader would rather be happy than unhappy. Whether I can help him to realize this wish, I do not know; but at any rate the attempt can do no harm.

CHAPTER II

Byronic Unhappiness

It is common in our day, as it has been in many other periods of the world's history, to suppose that those among us who are wise have seen through all the enthusiasms of earlier times and have become aware that there is nothing left to live for. The men who hold this view are genuinely unhappy, but they are proud of their unhappiness, which they attribute to the nature of the universe and consider to be the only rational attitude for an enlightened man. Their pride in their unhappiness makes less sophisticated people suspicious of its genuineness; they think that the man who enjoys being miserable is not miserable. This view is too simple; undoubtedly there is some slight compensation in the feeling of superiority and insight which these sufferers have, but it is not sufficient to make up for the loss of simpler pleasures. I do not myself think that there is any superior rationality in being unhappy. The wise man will be as happy as circumstances permit and if he finds the contemplation of the universe painful beyond a point, he will contemplate something else instead. This is what I wish to prove in the present chapter. I wish to persuade the reader that, whatever the arguments may be, reason lays no embargo upon happiness; nay, more, I am persuaded that those who quite sincerely attribute their sorrows to their views about the universe are putting the cart before the horse: the truth is that they are unhappy for some reason of which they are not aware, and this unhappiness leads them to dwell upon the less agreeable characteristics of the world in which they live.

For modern Americans the point of view that I wish to consider has been set forth by Mr Joseph Wood Krutch in a book called *The Modern Temper*; for our grandfathers' generation it was set forth by Byron; for all time it was set forth by the writer of Ecclesiastes. Mr Krutch says: 'Ours is a lost cause and there is no place for us in the natural universe, but we are not, for all that, sorry to be human. We should rather die as men than live as animals.' Byron says:

There's not a joy the world can give like that it takes away,
When the glow of early thought declines in feeling's dull decay.

The author of Ecclesiastes says:

Wherefore I praised the dead which are already dead more than the living which are yet alive.

Yea, better is he than both they, which hath not yet been, who hath not seen the evil work that is done under the sun.

All these three pessimists arrived at these gloomy conclusions after reviewing the pleasures of life. Mr Krutch has lived in the most intellectual circles of New York; Byron swam the Hellespont and had innumerable love affairs; the author of Ecclesiastes was even more varied in his pursuit of pleasure: he tried wine, he tried music, 'and that of all sorts', he built pools of water, he had men-servants and maid-servants, and servants born in his house. Even in these circumstances his wisdom departed not from him. Nevertheless he saw that all is vanity, even wisdom.

And I gave my heart to know wisdom, and to know madness and folly: I perceived that this also is vexation of spirit.

For in much wisdom is much grief: and he that increaseth knowledge increaseth sorrow.

His wisdom seems to have annoyed him; he made unsuccessful efforts to get rid of it.

I said in mine heart, Go to now, I will prove thee with mirth, therefore enjoy pleasure: and, behold, this also is vanity.

But his wisdom remained with him.

Then I said in my heart, As it happeneth to the fool, so it happeneth even to me; and why was I then more wise? Then I said in my heart, that this also is vanity.

Therefore I hated life; because the work that is wrought under the sun is grievous unto me: for all is vanity and vexation of spirit.

It is fortunate for literary men that people no longer read anything written long ago, for if they did they would come to the conclusion that, whatever may be said about pools of water, the making of new books is certainly vanity. If we can show that the doctrine of Ecclesiastes is not the only one open to a wise man, we need not trouble ourselves much with the later expressions of the same mood. In an argument of this sort we must distinguish between a mood and its intellectual expression. There is no arguing with a mood; it can be changed by some fortunate event, or by a change in our bodily condition, but it cannot be changed by argument. I have frequently experienced myself the mood in which I felt that all is vanity; I have emerged from it not by means of any philosophy, but owing to some imperative necessity of action. If your child is ill, you may be unhappy, but you will not feel that all is vanity; you will feel that the restoring of the child to health is a matter to be attended to regardless of the question whether there is ultimate value in human life or not. A rich man may, and often does, feel that all is vanity, but if he should happen to lose his money, he would feel that his next meal was by no means vanity. The feeling is one born of a too easy satisfaction of natural needs. The human animal, like others, is adapted to a certain amount of struggle for life, and when by means of great wealth *homo sapiens* can gratify all his whims without effort, the mere absence of effort from his life removes an essential ingredient of happiness. The man who acquires easily things for which he feels only a very moderate desire concludes that the attainment of desire does not bring happiness. If he is of a philosophic disposition, he concludes that human life is essentially wretched, since the man who has all he wants is still unhappy. He forgets that to be without some of the things you want is an indispensable part of happiness.

So much for the mood. There are, however, also intellectual arguments in Ecclesiastes.

The rivers run into the sea; yet the sea is not full.
There is no new thing under the sun.
There is no remembrance of former things.
I hated all my labour which I had taken under the sun: because I should leave it unto the man that shall be after me.

If one were to attempt to set up these arguments in the style of a modern philosopher they would come to something like this: Man is perpetually toiling, and matter is perpetually in motion yet nothing abides, although the new thing that comes after it is in no way different from what has gone before. A man dies, and his heir reaps the benefits of his labours; the rivers run into the sea, but their waters are not permitted to stay there. Over and over again in an endless purposeless cycle men and things are born and die without improvement, without permanent achievement, day after day, year after year. The rivers, if they were wise, would stay where they are. Solomon, if he were wise, would not plant fruit trees of which his son is to enjoy the fruit.

But in another mood how different all this looks. No new thing under the sun? What about skyscrapers, aeroplanes, and the broadcast speeches of politicians? What did Solomon[1] know about such things? If he could have heard on the wireless the speech of the Queen of Sheba to her subjects on her return from his dominions, would it not have consoled him among his futile trees and pools? If he could have had a press-cutting agency to let him know what the newspapers said about the beauty of his architecture, the comforts of his harem, and the discomfitures of rival sages in argument with him, could he have gone on saying that there is no new thing under the sun? It may be that these things would not have wholly cured his pessimism, but he would have had to give it a new expression. Indeed, one of Mr Krutch's complaints of our time is that there are so many new things under the sun. If either the absence or the presence of novelty is equally annoying, it would hardly seem that either could be the true cause of despair. Again, take the fact that 'all the rivers run into the sea, yet the sea is not full; unto the place from whence the rivers come, thither they return again'. Regarded as ground for pessimism, this assumes that travel is unpleasant. People go to health resorts in the summer, yet return again unto the place whence they came. This does not prove that it is futile to go to health resorts in the summer. If the waters were endowed with feeling, they would probably enjoy the adventurous cycle after the manner of Shelley's *Cloud*. As for the painfulness of leaving things to one's heir, that is a matter that may be looked at from two points of view: from the point of view of the heir it is distinctly

---

[1] Ecclesiastes was not, of course, really written by Solomon, but it is convenient to allude to the author by this name.

less disastrous. Nor is the fact that all things pass in itself any ground for pessimism. If they were succeeded by worse things, that would be a ground, but if they are succeeded by better things, that is a reason for optimism. What are we to think if, as Solomon maintains, they are succeeded by things exactly like themselves? Does not this make the whole process futile? Emphatically not, unless the various stages of the cycle are themselves painful. The habit of looking to the future and thinking that the whole meaning of the present lies in what it will bring forth is a pernicious one. There can be no value in the whole unless there is value in the parts. Life is not to be conceived on the analogy of a melodrama in which the hero and heroine go through incredible misfortunes for which they are compensated by a happy ending. I live and have my day, my son succeeds me and has his day, his son in turn succeeds him. What is there in all this to make a tragedy about? On the contrary, if I lived for ever the joys of life would inevitably in the end lose their savour. As it is, they remain perennially fresh.

> I warmed both hands before the fire of life;
> It sinks, and I am ready to depart.

This attitude is quite as rational as that of indignation with death. If, therefore, moods were to be decided by reason, there would be quite as much reason for cheerfulness as for despair.

'Ecclesiastes' is tragic; Mr Krutch's *Modern Temper* is pathetic. Mr Krutch, at bottom, is sad because the old mediaeval certainties have crumbled, and also some that are of more recent origin. 'As for this present unhappy time,' he says, 'haunted by ghosts from a dead world and not yet at home in its own, its predicament is not unlike the predicament of the adolescent who has not yet learned to orient himself without reference to the mythology amid which his childhood was passed.' This statement is entirely correct as applied to a certain section of intellectuals, those, namely, who, having had a literary education, can know nothing of the modern world, and having throughout their youth been taught to base belief upon emotion, cannot divest themselves of that infantile desire for safety and protection which the world of science cannot gratify. Mr Krutch, like most other literary men, is obsessed with the idea that science has not fulfilled its promises. He does not, of course, tell us what these promises were, but he seems to think that sixty years ago men like Darwin and Huxley expected something of science which it has not given. I think this is an entire delusion, fostered by those writers and clergymen who do not wish their specialties to be thought of little value. That the world contains many pessimists at the present moment is true. There have always been many pessimists whenever there have been many people whose income has diminished. Mr Krutch, it is true, is an American, and American incomes, on the whole, have been increased by the War, but throughout the Continent of Europe the intellectual classes have suffered terribly, while the War itself gave everyone a sense of instability. Such social causes have a great deal more to do with the mood of an epoch than has its theory as to the nature of the world. Few ages have been more despairing than the thirteenth century, although that faith which Mr Krutch so regrets was then firmly entertained by everyone except the Emperor and a few great Italian nobles. Thus Roger Bacon says: 'For more sins reign in these days of ours than in any past age, and sin is incompatible with wisdom. Let us see all conditions in the world, and consider them diligently everywhere: we shall find boundless corruption, and first of all in the Head. . . . Lechery dishonours the whole court, and gluttony is lord of all. . . . If then this is done in the Head, how is it in the members? See the prelates: how they hunt after money and neglect the cure of souls. . . . Let us consider the Religious Orders: I exclude none from what I say. See how they are fallen, one and all, from their right state; and the new Orders (of Friars) are already horribly decayed from their first dignity. The whole clergy is intent upon pride, lechery, and avarice: and wheresoever clerks are gathered together, as at Paris and Oxford, they scandalize the whole laity with their wars and quarrels and other vices. . . . None care what is done, or how, by hook or by crook, provided only that each can fulfil his lust.' Concerning the pagan sages of antiquity, he says: 'Their lives were beyond all comparison better than ours, both in all decency and in contempt of the world, with all its delights and riches and honours; as all men may read in the works of Aristotle, Seneca, Tully, Avicenna, Alfarabius, Plato, Socrates, and others;

and so it was that they attained to the secrets of wisdom and found out all knowledge.'[1] Roger Bacon's opinion was that of all his literary contemporaries, not one of whom liked the age in which he found himself. I do not for a moment believe that this pessimism had any metaphysical cause. Its causes were war, poverty, and violence.

One of Mr Krutch's most pathetic chapters deals with the subject of love. It appears that the Victorians thought very highly of it, but that we with our modern sophistication have come to see through it. 'For the more skeptical of the Victorians, love performed some of the functions of the God whom they had lost. Faced with it, many of even the most hard-headed turned, for the moment, mystical. They found themselves in the presence of something which awoke in them that sense of reverence which nothing else claimed, and something to which they felt, even in the very depth of their being, that an unquestioning loyalty was due. For them love, like God, demanded all sacrifices; but like Him, also, it rewarded the believer by investing all the phenomena of life with a meaning not yet analysed away. We have grown used—more than they—to a Godless universe, but we are not yet accustomed to one which is loveless as well, and only when we have so become shall we realize what atheism really means.' It is curious how different the Victorian age looks to the young of our time from what it seemed when one was living in it. I remember two old ladies, both typical of certain aspects of the period, whom I knew well in my youth. One was a Puritan, and the other a Voltairean. The former regretted that so much poetry deals with love, which, she maintained, is an uninteresting subject. The latter remarked: 'Nobody can say anything against me, but I always say that it is not so bad to break the seventh commandment as the sixth, because at any rate it requires the consent of the other party.' Neither of these views was quite like what Mr Krutch presents as typically Victorian. His ideas are derived evidently from certain writers who were by no means in harmony with their environment. The best example, I suppose, is Robert Browning. I cannot, however, resist the conviction that there is something stuffy about love as he conceived it.

[1] Quoted from Coulton's *From St. Francis to Dante*, p. 57.

God be thanked, the meanest of His creatures
Boasts two soul-sides, one to face the world with,
One to show a woman when he loves her!

This assumes that combativeness is the only possible attitude towards the world at large. Why? Because the world is cruel, Browning would say. Because it will not accept you at your own valuation, we should say. A couple may form, as the Brownings did, a mutual admiration society. It is very pleasant to have someone at hand who is sure to praise your work, whether it deserves it or not. And Browning undoubtedly felt that he was a fine, manly fellow when he denounced Fitzgerald in no measured terms for having dared not to admire Aurora Leigh. I cannot feel that this complete suspension of the critical faculty on both sides is really admirable. It is bound up with fear and with the desire to find a refuge from the cold blasts of impartial criticism. Many old bachelors learn to derive the same satisfaction from their own fireside. I lived too long myself in the Victorian age to be a modern according to Mr Krutch's standards. I have by no means lost my belief in love, but the kind of love that I can believe in is not the kind that the Victorians admired; it is adventurous and open-eyed, and, while it gives knowledge of good, it does not involve forgetfulness of evil, nor does it pretend to be sanctified or holy. The attribution of these qualities to the kind of love that was admired was an outcome of the sex taboo. The Victorian was profoundly convinced that most sex is evil, and had to attach exaggerated adjectives to the kind of which he could approve. There was more sex hunger than there is now, and this no doubt caused people to exaggerate the importance of sex just as the ascetics have always done. We are at the present day passing through a somewhat confused period, when many people have thrown over the old standards without acquiring new ones. This leads them into various troubles, and as their unconscious usually still believes in the old standards, the troubles, when they come, produce despair, remorse, and cynicism. I do not think the number of people to whom this happens is very large, but they are among the most vocal people of our time. I believe that if one took the average of well-to-do young people in our day and in the Victorian epoch, one would find that there is now a great deal more happiness in connection with love, and a great deal more genuine belief in the value of love than there was sixty years ago. The reasons which lead certain persons to cynicism are connected with the tyranny of the old ideals over the unconscious, and with the absence of a rational ethic by which present-day people can regulate their conduct. The cure lies not in lamentation and nostalgia for the past, but in a more courageous acceptance of the modern outlook and a determination to root out nominally discarded superstitions from all their obscure hiding places.

To say shortly why one values love is not easy; nevertheless, I will make the attempt. Love is to be valued in the first instance—and this, though not its greatest value, is essential to all the rest—as in itself a source of delight.

> Oh Love! they wrong thee much
> That say thy sweet is bitter,
> When thy rich fruit is such
> As nothing can be sweeter.

The anonymous author of these lines was not seeking a solution for atheism, or a key to the universe; he was merely enjoying himself. And not only is love a source of delight, but its absence is a source of pain. In the second place, love is to be valued because it enhances all the best pleasures, such as music, and sunrise in mountains, and the sea under the full moon. A man who has never enjoyed beautiful things in the company of a woman whom he loved has not experienced to the full the magic power of which such things are capable. Again, love is able to break down the hard shell of the ego, since it is a form of biological co-operation in which the emotions of each are necessary to the fulfilment of the other's instinctive purposes. There have been in the world at various times various solitary philosophies, some very noble, some less so. The Stoics and the early Christians believed that a man could realize the highest good of which human life is capable by means of his own will alone, or at any rate without *human* aid; others again have regarded power as the end of life, and yet others mere personal pleasure. All these are solitary philosophies in the sense that the good is supposed to be something realizable in each separate person, not only in a larger or smaller society of persons. All such views, to my mind, are false, and not only in ethical theory, but as expressions of the better part of our instincts. Man depends upon co-operation, and has been provided by nature, somewhat inadequately, it is true, with the instinctive apparatus out of which the friendliness required for co-operation can spring. Love is the first and commonest form of emotion leading to co-operation, and those who have experienced love with any intensity will not be content with a philosophy that supposes their highest good to be independent of that of the person loved. In this respect parental feeling is even more powerful, but parental feeling at its best is the result of love between the parents. I do not pretend that love in its highest form is common, but I do maintain that in its highest form it reveals values which must otherwise remain unknown, and has itself a value which is untouched by scepticism, although sceptics who are incapable of it may falsely attribute their incapacity to their scepticism.

> True love is a durable fire,
> In the mind ever burning,
> Never sick, never dead, never cold,
> From itself never turning.

I come next to what Mr Krutch has to say about tragedy. He contends, and in this I cannot but agree with him, that Ibsen's *Ghosts* is inferior to *King Lear*. 'No increased powers of expression, no greater gift for words, could have transformed Ibsen into Shakespeare. The materials out of which the latter created his works—his conception of human dignity, his sense of the importance of human passions, his vision of the amplitude of human life —simply did not and could not exist for Ibsen, as they did not and could not exist for his contemporaries. God and Man and Nature had all somehow dwindled in the course of the intervening centuries, not because the realistic creed of modern art led us to seek out mean people, but because this meanness of human life was somehow thrust upon us by the operation of that same process which led to the development of realistic theories of art by which our vision could be justified.' It is undoubtedly the case that the old-fashioned kind of tragedy which dealt with princes and their sorrows is not suitable to our age, and when we try to treat in the same manner the sorrows of an obscure individual the effect is not the same. The reason of this is not, however, any deterioration in our outlook on life, but quite the reverse. It is due to the fact that we can no longer regard certain individuals as the great ones of the earth, who have a right to tragic passions, while all the rest must merely drudge and toil to produce the magnificence of those few. Shakespeare says:

> When beggars die, there are no comets seen;
> The heavens themselves blaze forth the death of princes.

In Shakespeare's day this sentiment, if not literally believed, at least expressed an outlook which was practically universal and most profoundly accepted by Shakespeare himself. Consequently the death of Cinna the poet is comic, whereas the deaths of Caesar, Brutus and Cassius are tragic. The cosmic significance of an individual death is lost to us because we have become democratic, not only in outward forms, but in our inmost convictions. High tragedy in the present day, therefore, has to concern itself rather with the community than with the individual. I would give as an example of what I mean Ernst Toller's *Massemensch*.[1] I do not maintain that this work is as good as the best that has been done in the best ages in the past, but I do maintain that it is justly comparable; it is noble, profound and actual, concerned with heroic action, and 'purging the reader through pity and terror', as Aristotle said it should. There are as yet few examples of this modern kind of tragedy, since the old technique and the old traditions have to be abandoned without being replaced by mere educated commonplace. To write tragedy, a man must feel tragedy. To feel tragedy, a man must be aware of the world in which he lives, not only with his mind, but with his blood and sinews. Mr Krutch talks throughout his book at intervals about despair, and one is touched by his heroic acceptance of a bleak world, but the bleakness is due to the fact that he and most literary men have not yet learnt to feel the old emotions in response to new stimuli. The stimuli exist, but not in literary

[1] Translated into English by Vera Meynell under the title *Masses and Man*.

coteries. Literary coteries have no vital contact with the life of the community, and such contact is necessary if men's feelings are to have the seriousness and depth within which both tragedy and true happiness proceed. To all the talented young men who wander about feeling that there is nothing in the world for them to do, I should say: 'Give up trying to write, and, instead, try not to write. Go out into the world; become a pirate, a king in Borneo, a labourer in Soviet Russia; give yourself an existence in which the satisfaction of elementary physical needs will occupy almost all your energies.' I do not recommend this course of action to everyone, but only to those who suffer from the disease which Mr Krutch diagnoses. I believe that, after some years of such an existence, the ex-intellectual will find that in spite of his efforts he can no longer refrain from writing, and when this time comes his writing will not seem to him futile.

CHAPTER III

Competition

IF you ask any man in America, or any man in business in England, what it is that most interferes with his enjoyment of existence, he will say: 'The struggle for life.' He will say this in all sincerity; he will believe it. In a certain sense it is true; yet in another, and that a very important sense, it is profoundly false. The struggle for life is a thing which does, of course, occur. It may occur to any of us if we are unfortunate. It occurred, for example, to Conrad's hero Falk, who found himself on a derelict ship, one of the two men among the crew who were possessed of fire-arms, with nothing to eat but the other men. When the two men had finished the meals upon which they could agree, a true struggle for life began. Falk won, but was ever after a vegetarian. Now that is not what the business man means when he speaks of the 'struggle for life'. It is an inaccurate phrase which he has picked up in order to give dignity to something essentially trivial. Ask him how many men he has known in his class of life who have died of hunger. Ask him what happened to his friends after they had been ruined. Everybody knows that a business man who has been ruined is better off so far as material comforts are concerned than a man who has never been rich enough to have the chance of being ruined. What people mean, therefore, by the struggle for life is really the struggle for success. What people fear when they engage in the struggle is not that they will fail to get their breakfast next morning, but that they will fail to outshine their neighbours.

It is very singular how little men seem to realize that they are not caught in the grip of a mechanism from which there is no escape, but that the treadmill is one upon which they remain merely because they have not noticed that it fails to take them up to a higher level. I am thinking, of course, of men in higher walks of business, men who already have a good income and could, if they chose, live on what they have. To do so would seem to them shameful, like deserting from the army in the face of the enemy, though if you ask them what public cause they are serving by their work, they will be at a loss to reply as soon as they have run through the platitudes to be found in the advertisements of the strenuous life.

Consider the life of such a man. He has, we may suppose, a charming house, a charming wife, and charming children. He wakes up early in the morning while they are still asleep and hurries off to his office. There it is his duty to display the qualities of a great executive; he cultivates a firm jaw, a decisive manner of speech, and an air of sagacious reserve calculated to impress everybody except the office boy. He dictates letters, converses with various important persons on the 'phone, studies the market, and presently has lunch with some person with whom he is conducting or hoping to conduct a deal. The same sort of thing goes on all the afternoon. He arrives home, tired, just in time to dress for dinner. At dinner he and a number of other tired men have to pretend to enjoy the company of ladies who have no occasion to feel tired yet. How many hours it may take the poor man to escape it is impossible to foresee. At last he sleeps, and for a few hours the tension is relaxed.

The working life of this man has the psychology of a hundred-yards race, but as the race upon which he is engaged is one whose only goal is the grave, the concentration, which is appropriate enough for a hundred yards, becomes in the end somewhat excessive. What does he know about his children? On week-days he is at the office; on Sundays he is at the golf links. What does he know of his wife? When he leaves her in the morning, she is asleep. Throughout the evening he and she are engaged in social duties which prevent intimate conversation. He has probably no men friends who are important to him, although he has a number with whom he affects a geniality that he wishes he felt. Of springtime and harvest he knows only as they affect the market; foreign countries he has probably seen, but with eyes of utter boredom. Books seem to him futile, and music highbrow. Year by year he grows more lonely; his attention grows more concentrated and his life outside business more desiccated. I have seen the American of this type in later middle life, in Europe, with his wife and daughters. Evidently they had persuaded the poor fellow that it was time he took a holiday, and gave his girls a chance to do the Old World. The mother and daughters in ecstasy surround him and call his attention to each new item that strikes them as characteristic. Paterfamilias, utterly weary, utterly bored, is wondering what they are doing in the office at this moment, or what is happening in the baseball world. His womenkind, in the end, give him up, and conclude that males are Philistines. It never dawns upon them that he is a victim to their greed; nor, indeed, is this quite the truth, any more than suttee is quite what it appeared to a European onlooker. Probably in nine cases out of ten the widow was a willing victim, prepared to be burnt for the sake of glory and because religion so ordained. The business man's religion and glory demand that he should make much money; therefore, like the Hindu widow, he suffers the torment gladly. If the American business man is to be made happier, he must first change his religion. So long as he not only desires success, but is wholeheartedly persuaded that it is a man's duty to pursue success, and that a man who does not do so is a poor creature, so long his life will remain too concentrated and too anxious to be happy. Take a simple matter, such as investments. Almost every American would sooner get 8 per cent. from a risky investment than 4 per cent. from a safe one. The consequence is that there are frequent losses of money and continual worry and fret. For my part, the thing that I would wish to obtain from money would be leisure with security. But what the typical modern man desires to get with it is more money, with a view to ostentation, splendour, and the outshining of those who have hitherto been his equals. The social scale in America is indefinite and continually fluctuating. Consequently all the snobbish emotions become more restless than they are where the social order is fixed, and although money in itself may not suffice to make people grand, it is difficult to be grand without money. Moreover, money made is the accepted measure of brains. A man who makes a lot of money is a clever fellow; a man who does not, is not. Nobody likes to be thought a fool. Therefore, when the market is in ticklish condition, a man feels the way young people feel during an examination.

I think it should be admitted that an element of genuine though irrational fear as to the consequences of ruin frequently enters into a business man's anxieties. Arnold Bennett's Clayhanger, however rich he became, continued to be afraid of dying in the workhouse. I have no doubt that those who have suffered greatly through poverty in their childhood are haunted by terrors lest their children should suffer similarly, and feel that it is hardly possible to build up enough millions as a bulwark against this disaster. Such fears are probably inevitable in the first generation, but they are less likely to afflict those who have never known great poverty. They are in any case a minor and somewhat exceptional factor in the problem.

The root of the trouble springs from too much emphasis upon competitive success as the main source of happiness. I do not deny that the feeling of success makes it easier to enjoy life. A painter, let us say, who has been obscure throughout his youth, is likely to become happier if his talent wins recognition. Nor do I deny that money, up to a certain point, is very capable of increasing happiness; beyond that point, I do not think it does so. What I do maintain is that success can only be one ingredient in happiness, and is too dearly purchased if all the other ingredients have been sacrificed to obtain it.

The source of this trouble is the prevalent philosophy of life in business circles. In Europe, it is true, there are still other circles that have prestige. In some countries there is an aristocracy; in all there are the learned professions, and in all but a few of the smaller countries the army and the navy enjoy great respect. Now while it is true that there is a competitive element in success no matter what a man's profession may be, yet at the same time the kind of thing that is respected is not just success, but that excellence, whatever that may be, to which success has been due. A man of science may or may not make money; he is certainly not more respected if he does than if he does not. No one is surprised to find an eminent general or admiral poor; indeed, poverty in such circumstances is, in a sense, itself an honour. For these reasons, in Europe, the purely monetary competitive struggle is confined to certain circles, and those perhaps not the most influential or the most respected. In America the matter is otherwise. The Services play too small a part in the national life for their standards to have

B

any influence. As for the learned professions, no outsider can tell whether a doctor really knows much medicine, or whether a lawyer really knows much law, and it is therefore easier to judge of their merit by the income to be inferred from their standard of life. As for professors, they are the hired servants of business men, and as such win less respect than is accorded to them in older countries. The consequence of all this is that in America the professional man imitates the business man, and does not constitute a separate type as he does in Europe. Throughout the well-to-do classes, therefore, there is nothing to mitigate the bare undiluted fight for financial success.

From quite early years American boys feel that this is the only thing that matters, and do not wish to be bothered with any kind of education that is devoid of pecuniary value. Education used to be conceived very largely as a training in the capacity for enjoyment—enjoyment, I mean, of those more delicate kinds that are not open to wholly uncultivated people. In the eighteenth century it was one of the marks of a 'gentleman' to take a discriminating pleasure in literature, pictures, and music. We nowadays may disagree with his taste, but it was at least genuine. The rich man of the present day tends to be of quite a different type. He never reads. If he is creating a picture gallery with a view to enhancing his fame, he relies upon experts to choose his pictures; the pleasure that he derives from them is not the pleasure of looking at them, but the pleasure of preventing some other rich man from having them. In regard to music, if he happens to be a Jew, he may have genuine appreciation; if not, he will be as uncultivated as he is in regard to the other arts. The result of all this is that he does not know what to do with leisure. As he gets richer and richer it become easier and easier to make money, until at last five minutes a day will bring him more than he knows how to spend. The poor man is thus left at a loose end as a result of his success. This must inevitably be the case so long as success itself is represented as the purpose of life. Unless a man has been taught what to do with success after getting it, the achievement of it must inevitably leave him a prey to boredom.

The competitive habit of mind easily invades regions to which it does not belong. Take, for example, the question of reading.

There are two motives for reading a book: one, that you enjoy it; the other, that you can boast about it. It has become the thing in America for ladies to read (or seem to read) certain books every month; some read them, some read the first chapter, some read the reviews, but all have these books on their tables. They do not, however, read any masterpieces. There has never been a month when *Hamlet* or *King Lear* has been selected by the Book Clubs; there has never been a month when it has been necessary to know about Dante. Consequently the reading that is done is entirely of mediocre modern books and never of masterpieces. This also is an effect of competition, not perhaps wholly bad, since most of the ladies in question, if left to themselves, so far from reading masterpieces, would read books even worse than those selected for them by their literary pastors and masters.

The emphasis upon competition in modern life is connected with a general decay of civilized standards such as must have occurred in Rome after the Augustan age. Men and women appear to have become incapable of enjoying the more intellectual pleasures. The art of general conversation, for example, brought to perfection in the French salons of the eighteenth century, was still a living tradition forty years ago. It was a very exquisite art, bringing the highest faculties into play for the sake of something completely evanescent. But who in our age cares for anything so leisurely? In China the art still flourished in perfection ten years ago, but I imagine that the missionary ardour of the Nationalists has since then swept it completely out of existence. The knowledge of good literature, which was universal among educated people fifty or a hundred years ago, is now confined to a few professors. All the quieter pleasures have been abandoned. Some American students took me walking in the spring through a wood on the borders of their campus; it was filled with exquisite wild flowers, but not one of my guides knew the name of even one of them. What use would such knowledge be? It could not add to anybody's income.

The trouble does not lie simply with the individual, nor can a single individual prevent it in his own isolated case. The trouble arises from the generally received philosophy of life, according to which life is a contest, a competition, in which respect is to be accorded to the victor. This view leads to an undue cultivation of the will at the expense of the senses and the intellect. Or possibly, in saying this, we may be putting the cart before the horse. Puritan moralists have always emphasized the will in modern times, although originally it was faith upon which they laid stress. It may be that ages of Puritanism produced a race in which will had been overdeveloped, while the senses and the intellect had been starved, and that such a race adopted a philosophy of competition as the one best suited to its nature. However that may be, the prodigious success of these modern dinosaurs, who, like their prehistoric prototypes, prefer power to intelligence, is causing them to be universally imitated: they have become the pattern for the white man everywhere, and this is likely to be increasingly the case for the next hundred years. Those, however, who are not in the fashion may take comfort from the thought that the dinosaurs did not ultimately triumph; they killed each other out, and intelligent bystanders inherited their kingdom. Our modern dinosaurs are killing themselves out. They do not, on the average, have so much as two children per marriage; they do not enjoy life enough to wish to beget children. At this point the unduly strenuous philosophy which they have carried over from their Puritan forefathers shows itself unadapted to the world. Those whose outlook on life causes them to feel so little happiness that they do not care to beget children are biologically doomed. Before very long they must be succeeded by something gayer and jollier.

Competition considered as the main thing in life is too grim, too tenacious, too much a matter of taut muscles and intent will, to make a possible basis of life for more than one or two generations at most. After that length of time it must produce nervous fatigue, various phenomena of escape, a pursuit of pleasures as tense and as difficult as work (since relaxing has become impossible), and in the end a disappearance of the stock through sterility. It is not only work that is poisoned by the philosophy of competition; leisure is poisoned just as much. The kind of leisure which is quiet and restoring to the nerves comes to be felt boring. There is bound to be a continual acceleration of which the natural termination would be drugs and collapse. The cure for this lies in admitting the part of sane and quiet enjoyment in a balanced ideal of life.

CHAPTER IV

Boredom and Excitement

BOREDOM as a factor in human behaviour has received, in my opinion, far less attention than it deserves. It has been, I believe, one of the great motive powers throughout the historical epoch, and is so at the present day more than ever. Boredom would seem to be a distinctively human emotion. Animals in captivity, it is true, become listless, pace up and down, and yawn, but in a state of nature I do not believe that they experience anything analogous to boredom. Most of the time they are on the look-out for enemies, or food, or both; sometimes they are mating, sometimes they are trying to keep warm. But even when they are unhappy, I do not think that they are bored. Possibly anthropoid apes may resemble us in this respect, as in so many others, but having never lived with them I have not had the opportunity to make the experiment. One of the essentials of boredom consists in the contrast between present circumstances and some other more agreeable circumstances which force themselves irresistibly upon the imagination. It is also one of the essentials of boredom that one's faculties must not be fully occupied. Running away from enemies who are trying to take one's life is, I imagine, unpleasant, but certainly not boring. A man would not feel bored while he was being executed, unless he had almost superhuman courage. In like manner no one has ever yawned during his maiden speech in the House of Lords, with the exception of the late Duke of Devonshire, who was reverenced by their Lordships in consequence. Boredom is essentially a thwarted desire for events, not necessarily pleasant ones, but just occurrences such as will enable the victim of *ennui* to know one day from another. The opposite of boredom, in a word, is not pleasure, but excitement.

The desire for excitement is very deep-seated in human beings, especially in males. I suppose that in the hunting stage it was more easily gratified than it has been since. The chase was exciting, war was exciting, courtship was exciting. A savage will manage to commit adultery with a woman while her husband is asleep beside her, knowing that it is instant death if the husband wakes. This situation, I imagine, is not boring. But with the coming of agriculture life began to grow dull, except, of course, for the aristocrats, who remained, and still remain, in the hunting stage. We hear a great deal about the tedium of machine-minding, but I think the tedium of agriculture by old-fashioned methods is at least as great. Indeed, contrary to what most philanthropists maintain, I should say that the machine age has enormously diminished the sum of boredom in the world. Among wage-earners the working hours are not solitary, while the evening hours can be given over to a variety of amusements that were impossible in an old-fashioned country village. Consider again the change in lower middle-class life. In old days, after supper, when the wife and daughters had cleared away the things, everybody sat round and had what was called 'a happy family time'. This meant that paterfamilias went to sleep, his wife knitted, and the daughters wished they were dead or at Timbuktu. They were not allowed to read, or to leave the room, because the theory was that at that period their father conversed with them, which must be a pleasure to all concerned. With luck they ultimately married and had a chance to inflict upon their children a youth as dismal as their own had been. If they did not have luck, they developed into old maids, perhaps ultimately into decayed gentlewomen—a fate as horrible as any that savages have bestowed upon their victims. All this weight of boredom should be borne in mind in estimating the world of a hundred years ago, and when one goes further into the past the boredom becomes still worse. Imagine the monotony of winter in a mediaeval village. People could not read or write, they had only candles to give them light after dark, the smoke of their one fire filled the only room that was not bitterly cold. Roads were practically impassable, so that one hardly ever saw anybody from another village. It must have been boredom as much as anything that led to the practice of witch hunts as the sole sport by which winter evenings could be enlivened.

We are less bored than our ancestors were, but we are more afraid of boredom. We have come to know, or rather to believe, that boredom is not part of the natural lot of man, but can be avoided by a sufficiently vigorous pursuit of excitement. Girls nowadays earn their own living, very largely because this enables them to seek excitement in the evening and to escape 'the happy family time' that their grandmothers had to endure. Everybody who can lives in a town; in America, those who cannot, have a car, or at the least a motor-bicycle, to take them to the movies. And of course they have the radio in their houses. Young men and young women meet each other with much less difficulty than was formerly the case, and every housemaid expects at least once a week as much excitement as would have lasted a Jane Austen heroine throughout a whole novel. As we rise in the social scale the pursuit of excitement becomes more and more intense. Those who can afford it are perpetually moving from place to place, carrying with them as they go gaiety, dancing and drinking, but for some reason always expecting to enjoy these more in a new place. Those who have to earn a living get their share of boredom, of necessity, in working hours, but those who have enough money to be freed from the need of work have as their ideal a life completely freed from boredom. It is a noble ideal, and far be it from me to decry it, but I am afraid that like other ideals it is more difficult of achievement than the idealists suppose. After all, the mornings are boring in proportion as the previous evenings were amusing. There will be middle age, possibly even old age. At twenty men think that life will be over at thirty. I, at the age of fifty-eight, can no longer take that view. Perhaps it is as unwise to spend one's vital capital as one's financial capital. Perhaps some element of boredom is a necessary ingredient in life. A wish to escape from boredom is natural; indeed, all races of mankind have displayed it as opportunity occurred. When savages have first tasted liquor at the hands of the white men, they have found at last an escape from age-old tedium, and, except when the Government has interfered, they have drunk themselves into a riotous death. Wars, pogroms, and persecutions have all been part of the flight from boredom; even quarrels with neighbours have been found better than nothing. Boredom is therefore a vital problem for the moralist, since at least half the sins of mankind are caused by the fear of it.

Boredom, however, is not to be regarded as wholly evil. There are two sorts, of which one is fructifying, while the other is stultifying. The fructifying kind arises from the absence of drugs, and the stultifying kind from the absence of vital activities. I am not prepared to say that drugs can play no good part in life whatsoever. There are moments, for example, when an opiate will be prescribed by a wise physician, and I think these moments more frequent than prohibitionists suppose. But the craving for drugs is certainly something which cannot be left to the unfettered operation of natural impulse. And the kind of boredom which the person accustomed to drugs experiences when deprived of them is something for which I can suggest no remedy except time. Now what applies to drugs applies also, within limits, to every kind of excitement. A life too full of excitement is an exhausting life, in which continually stronger stimuli are needed to give the thrill that has come to be thought an essential part of pleasure. A person accustomed to too much excitement is like a person with a morbid craving for pepper, who comes at last to be unable even to taste a quantity of pepper which would cause anyone else to choke. There is an element of boredom which is inseparable from the avoidance of too much excitement, and too much excitement not only undermines the health, but dulls the palate for every kind of pleasure, substituting titillations for profound organic satisfactions, cleverness for wisdom, and jagged surprises for beauty. I do not want to push to extremes the objection to excitement. A certain amount of it is wholesome, but, like almost everything else, the matter is quantitative. Too little may produce morbid cravings, too much will produce exhaustion. A certain power of enduring boredom is therefore essential to a happy life, and is one of the things that ought to be taught to the young.

All great books contain boring portions, and all great lives have contained uninteresting stretches. Imagine a modern American publisher confronted with the Old Testament as a new manuscript submitted to him for the first time. It is not difficult to think what his comments would be, for example, on the genealogies.

'My dear sir,' he would say, 'this chapter lacks pep; you can't expect your reader to be interested in a mere string of proper names of persons about whom you tell him so little. You have begun your story, I will admit, in fine style, and at first I was very favourably impressed, but you have altogether too much wish to tell it all. Pick out the high lights, take out the superfluous matter, and bring me back your manuscript when you have reduced it to a reasonable length.' So the modern publisher would speak, knowing the modern reader's fear of boredom. He would say the same sort of thing about the Confucian classics, the Koran, Marx's *Capital*, and all the other sacred books which have proved to be best sellers. Nor does this apply only to sacred books. All the best novels contain boring passages. A novel which sparkles from the first page to the last is pretty sure not to be a great book. Nor have the lives of great men been exciting except at a few great moments. Socrates could enjoy a banquet now and again, and must have derived considerable satisfaction from his conversations while the hemlock was taking effect, but most of his life he lived quietly with Xanthippe, taking a constitutional in the afternoon, and perhaps meeting a few friends by the way. Kant is said never to have been more than ten miles from Königsberg in all his life. Darwin, after going round the world, spent the whole of the rest of his life in his own house. Marx, after stirring up a few revolutions, decided to spend the remainder of his days in the British Museum. Altogether it will be found that a quiet life is characteristic of great men, and that their pleasures have not been of the sort that would look exciting to the outward eye. No great achievement is possible without persistent work, so absorbing and so difficult that little energy is left over for the more strenuous kinds of amusement, except such as serve to recuperate physical energy during holidays, of which Alpine climbing may serve as the best example.

The capacity to endure a more or less monotonous life is one which should be acquired in childhood. Modern parents are greatly to blame in this respect; they provide their children with far too many passive amusements, such as shows and good things to eat, and they do not realize the importance to a child of having one day like another, except, of course, for somewhat rare occasions. The pleasures of childhood should in the main be such as the child extracts from his environment by means of some effort and inventiveness. Pleasures which are exciting and at the same time involve no physical exertion, such, for example, as the theatre, should occur very rarely. The excitement is in the nature of a drug, of which more and more will come to be required, and the physical passivity during the excitement is contrary to instinct. A child develops best when, like a young plant, he is left undisturbed in the same soil. Too much travel, too much variety of impressions, are not good for the young, and cause them as they grow up to become incapable of enduring fruitful monotony. I do not mean that monotony has any merits of its own; I mean only that certain good things are not possible except where there is a certain degree of monotony. Take, say, Wordsworth's *Prelude*. It will be obvious to every reader that whatever had any value in Wordsworth's thoughts and feelings would have been impossible to a sophisticated urban youth. A boy or young man who has some serious constructive purpose will endure voluntarily a great deal of boredom if he finds that it is necessary by the way. But constructive purposes do not easily form themselves in a boy's mind if he is living a life of distractions and dissipations, for in that case his thoughts will always be directed towards the next pleasure rather than towards the distant achievement. For all these reasons a generation that cannot endure boredom will be a generation of little men, of men unduly divorced from the slow processes of nature, of men in whom every vital impulse slowly withers, as though they were cut flowers in a vase.

I do not like mystical language, and yet I hardly know how to express what I mean without employing phrases that sound poetic rather than scientific. Whatever we may wish to think, we are creatures of Earth; our life is part of the life of the Earth, and we draw our nourishment from it just as the plants and animals do. The rhythm of Earth life is slow; autumn and winter are as essential to it as spring and summer, and rest is as essential as motion. To the child, even more than to the man, it is necessary to preserve some contact with the ebb and flow of terrestrial life. The human body has been adapted through the ages to this rhythm, and religion has embodied something of it in the festival of Easter. I have seen a boy of two years old, who had been kept in London, taken out for the first time to walk in green country. The season was winter, and everything was wet and muddy. To the adult eye there was nothing to cause delight, but in the boy there sprang up a strange ecstasy; he kneeled in the wet ground and put his face in the grass, and gave utterance to half-articulate cries of delight. The joy that he was experiencing was primitive, simple and massive. The organic need that was being satisfied is so profound that those in whom it is starved are seldom completely sane. Many pleasures, of which we may take gambling as a good example, have in them no element of this contact with Earth. Such pleasures, in the instant when they cease, leave a man feeling dusty and dissatisfied, hungry for he knows not what. Such pleasures bring nothing that can be called joy. Those, on the other hand, that bring us into contact with the life of the Earth have something in them profoundly satisfying; when they cease, the happiness that they brought remains, although their intensity while they existed may have been less than that of more exciting dissipations. The distinction that I have in mind runs through the whole gamut from the simplest to the most civilized occupations. The two-year-old boy whom I spoke of a moment ago displayed the most primitive possible form of union with the life of Earth. But in a higher form the same thing is to be found in poetry. What makes Shakespeare's lyrics supreme is that they are filled with this same joy that made the two-year-old embrace the grass. Consider 'Hark, hark, the lark', or 'Come unto these yellow sands'; you will find in these poems the civilized expression of the same emotion that in our two-year-old could only find utterance in inarticulate cries. Or, again, consider the difference between love and mere sex attraction. Love is an experience in which our whole being is renewed and refreshed as is that of plants by rain after drought. In sex intercourse without love there is nothing of this. When the momentary pleasure is ended, there is fatigue, disgust, and a sense that life is hollow. Love is part of the life of Earth; sex without love is, not.

The special kind of boredom from which modern urban populations suffer is intimately bound up with their separation from the life of Earth. It makes life hot and dusty and thirsty, like a pilgrimage in the desert. Among those who are rich enough to choose their way of life, the particular brand of unendurable boredom from which they suffer is due, paradoxical as this may seem, to their fear of boredom. In flying from the fructifying kind of boredom, they fall a prey to the other far worse kind. A happy life must be to a great extent a quiet life, for it is only in an atmosphere of quiet that true joy can live.

CHAPTER V

Fatigue

FATIGUE is of many sorts, some of which are a much graver obstacle to happiness than others. Purely physical fatigue, provided it is not excessive, tends if anything to be a cause of happiness; it leads to sound sleep and a good appetite, and gives zest to the pleasures that are possible on holidays. But when it is excessive it becomes a very grave evil. Peasant women in all but the most advanced communities are old at thirty, worn out with excessive toil. Children in the early days of industrialism were stunted in their growth and frequently killed by overwork in early years. The same thing still happens in China and Japan, where industrialism is new; to some extent also in the Southern States of America. Physical labour carried beyond a certain point is atrocious torture, and it has very frequently been carried so far as to make life all but unbearable. In the most advanced parts of the modern world, however, physical fatigue has been much minimized through the improvement of industrial conditions. The kind of fatigue that is most serious in the present day in advanced communities is nervous fatigue. This kind, oddly enough, is most pronounced among the well-to-do, and tends to be much less among wage-earners than it is among business men and brain-workers.

To escape from nervous fatigue in modern life is a very difficult thing. In the first place, all through working hours, and still more in the time spent between work and home, the urban worker is exposed to noise, most of which, it is true, he learns not to hear consciously, but which none the less wears him out, all the more owing to the subconscious effort involved in not hearing it. Another thing which causes fatigue without our being aware of it is the constant presence of strangers. The natural instinct of man, as of other animals, is to investigate every stranger of his species, with a view to deciding whether to behave to him in a friendly or hostile manner. This instinct has to be inhibited by those who travel in the underground in the rush hour, and the result of inhibiting it is that they feel a general diffused rage against all the strangers with whom they are brought into this involuntary contact. Then there is the hurry to catch the morning train, with the resulting dyspepsia. Consequently, by the time the office is reached and the day's work begins, the black-coated worker already has frayed nerves and a tendency to view the human race as a nuisance. His employer, arriving in the same mood, does nothing to dissipate it in the employee. Fear of the sack compels respectful behaviour, but this unnatural conduct only adds to the nervous strain. If once a week employees were allowed to pull the employer's nose and otherwise indicate what they thought of him, the nervous tension for them would be relieved, but for the employer, who also has his troubles, this would not mend matters. What the fear of dismissal is to the employee, the fear of bankruptcy is to the employer. Some, it is true, are big enough to be above this fear, but to reach a great position of this kind they have generally had to pass through years of strenuous struggle, during which they had to be actively aware of events in all parts of the world and constantly foiling the machinations of their competitors. The result of all this is that when sound success comes a man is already a nervous wreck, so accustomed to anxiety that he cannot shake off the habit of it when the need for it is past. There are, it is true, rich men's sons, but they generally succeed in manufacturing for themselves anxieties as similar as possible to those that they would have suffered if they had not been born rich. By betting and gambling, they incur the displeasure of their fathers; by cutting short their sleep for the sake of their amusements, they debilitate their physique; and by the time they settle down, they have become as incapable of happiness as their fathers were before them. Voluntarily or involuntarily, of choice or of necessity, most moderns lead a nerve-racking life, and are continually too tired to be capable of enjoyment without the help of alcohol.

Leaving on one side those rich men who are merely fools, let us consider the commoner case of those whose fatigue is associated with strenuous work for a living. To a great extent fatigue in such cases is due to worry, and worry could be prevented by a better philosophy of life and a little more mental discipline. Most men and women are very deficient in control over their thoughts. I mean by this that they cannot cease to think about worrying topics at times when no action can be taken in regard to them. Men take their business worries to bed with them, and in the hours of the night, when they should be gaining fresh strength to cope with tomorrow's troubles, they are going over and over again in their minds problems about which at the moment they can do nothing, thinking about them, not in a way to produce a sound line of conduct on the morrow, but in that half-insane way that characterizes the troubled meditations of insomnia. Something of the midnight madness still clings about them in the morning, clouding their judgment, spoiling their temper, and making every obstacle infuriating. The wise man thinks about his troubles only when there is some purpose in doing so; at other times he thinks about other things, or, if it is night, about nothing at all. I do not mean to suggest that at a great crisis, for example, when ruin is imminent, or when a man has reason to suspect that his wife is deceiving him, it is possible, except to a few exceptionally disciplined minds, to shut out the trouble at moments when nothing can be done about it. But it is quite possible to shut out the ordinary troubles of ordinary days, except while they have to be dealt with. It is amazing how much both happiness and efficiency can be increased by the cultivation of an orderly mind, which thinks about a matter adequately at the right time rather than inadequately at all times. When a difficult or worrying decision has to be reached, as soon as all the data are available give the matter your best thought and make your decision; having made the decision, do not revise it unless some new fact comes to your knowledge. Nothing is so exhausting as indecision, and nothing is so futile.

A great many worries can be diminished by realizing the unimportance of the matter which is causing the anxiety. I have done in my time a considerable amount of public speaking; at first every audience terrified me, and nervousness made me speak very badly; I dreaded the ordeal so much that I always hoped I might break my leg before I had to make a speech, and when it was over I was exhausted from the nervous strain. Gradually I taught myself to feel that it did not matter whether I spoke well or ill, the universe would remain much the same in either case. I found that the less I cared whether I spoke well or badly, the less badly I spoke, and gradually the nervous strain diminished almost to vanishing point. A great deal of nervous fatigue can be dealt with in this way. Our doings are not so important as we naturally suppose; our successes and failures do not after all matter very much. Even great sorrows can be survived; troubles which seem as if they must put an end to happiness for life fade with the lapse of time until it becomes almost impossible to remember their poignancy. But over and above these self-centred considerations is the fact that one's ego is no very large part of the world. The man who can centre his thoughts and hopes upon something transcending self can find a certain peace in the ordinary troubles of life which is impossible to the pure egoist.

What might be called hygiene of the nerves has been much too little studied. Industrial psychology, it is true, has made elaborate investigations into fatigue, and has proved by careful statistics that if you go on doing something for a sufficiently long time you will ultimately get rather tired—a result which might have been guessed without so much parade of science. The study of fatigue by psychologists is mainly concerned with muscular fatigue, although there are also a certain number of studies of fatigue in school children. None of these, however, touch upon the important problem. The important kind of fatigue is always emotional in modern life; purely intellectual fatigue, like purely muscular fatigue, produces its own remedy in sleep. Any person who has a great deal of intellectual work devoid of emotion to do—say, for example, elaborate computations—will sleep off at the end of each day the fatigue that that day has brought. The harm that is attributed to overwork is hardly ever due to that cause, but to some kind of worry or anxiety The trouble with emotional fatigue is that it interferes with rest. The more tired a man becomes, the more impossible he finds it to stop. One of the symptoms of approaching nervous break-down is the belief that one's work is terribly important, and that to take a holiday would bring all kinds of disaster. If I were a medical man, I should prescribe a holiday to any patient who considered his work important. The nervous break-down which appears to be produced by the work is, in fact, in every case that I have ever known of personally, produced by some emotional trouble from which the patient attempts to escape by means of his work. He is loath to give up his work because, if he does so, he will no longer have anything to distract him from the thoughts of his misfortune, whatever it may be. Of course, the trouble may be fear of bankruptcy, and in that case his work is directly connected with his worry, but even then worry is likely to lead him to work so long that his judgment becomes clouded and bankruptcy comes sooner than if he worked less. In every case it is the emotional trouble, not the work, that causes the break-down.

The psychology of worry is by no means simple. I have spoken already of mental discipline, namely the habit of thinking of things at the right time. This has its importance, first because it makes it possible to get through the day's work with less expenditure of thought, secondly because it affords a cure for insomnia, and thirdly because it promotes efficiency and wisdom in decisions. But methods of this kind do not touch the subconscious or the unconscious, and when a trouble is grave no method is of much avail unless it penetrates below the level of consciousness. There has been a great deal of study by psychologists of the operation of the unconscious upon the conscious, but much less of the operation of the conscious upon the unconscious. Yet the latter is of vast importance in the subject of mental hygiene, and must be understood if rational convictions are ever to operate in the realm of the unconscious. This applies in particular in the matter of worry. It is easy enough to tell oneself that such and such a misfortune would not be so very terrible if it happened, but so long as this remains merely a conscious conviction it will not operate in the watches of the night, or prevent the occurrence of nightmares. My own belief is that a conscious thought can be planted into the unconscious if a sufficient amount of vigour and intensity is put into it. Most of the unconscious consists of what were once highly emotional conscious thoughts, which have now become buried. It is possible to do this process of burying deliberately, and in this way the unconscious can be led to do a lot of useful work. I have found, for example, that if I have to write upon some rather difficult topic the best plan is to think about it with very great intensity—the greatest intensity of which I am capable—for a few hours or days, and at the end of that time give orders, so to speak, that the work is to proceed underground. After some months I return consciously to the topic and find that the work has been done. Before I had discovered this technique, I used to spend the intervening months worrying because I was making no progress; I arrived at the solution none the sooner for this worry, and the intervening months were wasted, whereas now I can devote them to other pursuits. A process in many ways analogous can be adopted with regard to anxieties. When some misfortune threatens, consider seriously and deliberately what is the very worst that could possibly happen. Having looked this possible misfortune in the face, give yourself sound reasons for thinking that after all it would be no such very terrible disaster. Such reasons always exist, since at the worst nothing that happens to oneself has any cosmic importance. When you have looked for some time steadily at the worst possibility and have said to yourself with real conviction, 'Well, after all, that would not matter so very much', you will find that your worry diminishes to a quite extraordinary extent. It may be necessary to repeat the process a few times, but in the end, if you have shirked nothing in facing the worst possible issue, you will find that your worry disappears altogether, and is replaced by a kind of exhilaration.

This is part of a more general technique for the avoidance of fear. Worry is a form of fear, and all forms of fear produce fatigue. A man who has learnt not to feel fear will find the fatigue of daily life enormously diminished. Now fear, in its most harmful form, arises where there is some danger which we are unwilling to face. At odd moments horrible thoughts dart into our minds; what they are depends upon the person, but almost everybody has some kind of lurking fear. With one man it is cancer, with another financial ruin, with a third the discovery of some disgraceful secret, a fourth is tormented by jealous suspicions, a fifth is haunted at night by the thought that perhaps the tales of hell-fire told him when he was young may be true. Probably all these people employ the wrong technique for dealing with their fear; whenever it comes into their mind, they try to think of something else; they distract their thoughts with amusement or work, or what not. Now every kind of fear grows worse by not being looked at. The effort of turning away one's thoughts is a tribute to the horribleness of the spectre from which one is averting one's gaze; the proper course with every kind of fear is to think about it rationally and calmly, but with great concentration, until it has become completely familiar. In the end familiarity will blunt its terrors; the whole subject will become boring, and our thoughts will turn away from it, not, as formerly, by an effort of will, but through mere lack of interest in the topic. When you find yourself inclined to brood on anything, no matter what, the best plan always is to think about it even more than you naturally would, until at last its morbid fascination is worn off.

One of the matters in which modern morality is most defective is this question of fear. It is true that physical courage, especially in war, is expected of men, but other forms of courage are not expected of them, and no form of courage is expected of women. A woman who is courageous has to conceal the fact if she wishes men to like her. The man who is courageous in any matter except physical danger is also thought ill of. Indifference to public opinion, for example, is regarded as a challenge, and the public does what it can to punish the man who dares to flout its authority. All this is quite opposite to what it should be. Every form of courage, whether in men or women, should be admired as much as physical courage is admired in a soldier. The commonness of physical courage among young men is a proof that courage can be produced in response to a public opinion that demands it. Given more courage there would be less worry, and therefore less fatigue; for a very large proportion of the nervous fatigues from which men and women suffer at present are due to fears, conscious or unconscious.

A very frequent source of fatigue is love of excitement. If a man could spend his leisure in sleep, he would keep fit, but his working hours are dreary, and he feels the need of pleasure during his hours of freedom. The trouble is that the pleasures which are easiest to obtain and most superficially attractive are mostly of a sort to wear out the nerves. Desire for excitement, when it goes beyond a point, is a sign either of a twisted disposition or of some instinctive dissatisfaction. In the early days of a happy marriage most men feel no need of excitement, but in the modern world marriage often has to be postponed for such a long time that when at last it becomes financially possible excitement has become a habit which can only be kept at bay for a short time. If public opinion allowed men to marry at twenty-one without incurring the financial burdens at present involved in matrimony, many men would never get into the way of demanding pleasures as fatiguing as their work. To suggest that this should be made possible is, however, immoral, as may be seen from the fate of Judge Lindsey, who has suffered obloquy, in spite of a long and honourable career, for the sole crime of wishing to save young people from the misfortunes that they incur as a result of their elders' bigotry. I shall not, however, pursue this topic any further at present, since it comes under the heading of Envy, with which we shall be concerned in a later chapter.

For the private individual, who cannot alter the laws and institutions under which he lives, it is difficult to cope with the situation that oppressive moralists created and perpetuate. It is, however, worth while to realize that exciting pleasures are not a road to happiness, although so long as more satisfying joys remain unattainable a man may find it hardly possible to endure life except by the help of excitement. In such a situation the only thing that a prudent man can do is to ration himself, and not to allow himself such an amount of fatiguing pleasure as will undermine his health or interfere with his work. The radical cure for the troubles of the young lies in a change of public morals. In the meantime a young man does well to reflect that he will ultimately be in a position to marry, and that he will be unwise if he lives in such a way as to make a happy marriage impossible, which may easily happen through frayed nerves and an acquired incapacity for the gentler pleasures.

One of the worst features of nervous fatigue is that it acts as a sort of screen between a man and the outside world. Impressions reach him, as it were, muffled and muted; he no longer notices people except to be irritated by small tricks or mannerisms; he derives no pleasure from his meals or from the sunshine, but tends to become tensely concentrated upon a few objects and indifferent to all the rest. This state of affairs makes it impossible to rest, so that fatigue continually increases until it reaches a point where medical treatment is required. All this is at bottom a penalty for having lost that contact with Earth of which we spoke in the preceding chapter. But how such contact is to be preserved in our great modern urban agglomerations of population, it is by no means easy to see. However, here again we find ourselves upon the fringe of large social questions with which in this volume it is not my intention to deal.

CHAPTER VI

Envy

———————•———————

NEXT to worry probably one of the most potent causes of un-happiness is envy. Envy is, I should say, one of the most universal and deep-seated of human passions. It is very noticeable in children before they are a year old, and has to be treated with the most tender respect by every educator. The very slightest appearance of favouring one child at the expense of another is instantly observed and resented. Distributive justice, absolute, rigid, and unvarying, must be observed by anyone who has children to deal with. But children are only slightly more open in their expressions of envy, and of jealousy (which is a special form of envy), than are grown-up people. The emotion is just as prevalent among adults as among children. Take, for example, maid-servants: I remember when one of our maids, who was a married woman, became pregnant, and we said that she was not to be expected to lift heavy weights, the instant result was that none of the others would lift heavy weights, and any work of that sort that needed doing we had to do ourselves. Envy is the basis of democracy. Heraclitus asserts that the citizens of Ephesus ought all to be hanged because they said, 'There shall be none first among us'. The democratic movement in Greek States must have been almost wholly inspired by this passion. And the same is true of modern democracy. There is, it is true, an idealistic theory according to which democracy is the best form of government. I think myself that this theory is true. But there is no department of practical politics where idealistic theories are strong enough to cause great changes; when great changes occur, the theories which justify them are always a camouflage for passion. And the passion that has given driving force to democratic theories is undoubtedly the passion of envy. Read the memoirs of Madame Roland, who is frequently repre-sented as a noble woman inspired by devotion to the people. You will find that what made her such a vehement democrat was the

experience of being shown into the servants' hall when she had
occasion to visit an aristocratic château.

Among average respectable women envy plays an extraordinarily large part. If you are sitting in the Underground and a
well-dressed woman happens to walk along the car, watch the eyes
of the other women. You will see that every one of them, with the
possible exception of those who are better dressed, will watch the
woman with malevolent glances, and will be struggling to draw
inferences derogatory to her. The love of scandal is an expression
of this general malevolence: any story against another woman is
instantly believed, even on the flimsiest evidence. A lofty morality
serves the same purpose: those who have a chance to sin against it
are envied, and it is considered virtuous to punish them for their
sins. This particular form of virtue is certainly its own reward.

Exactly the same thing, however, is to be observed among men,
except that women regard all other women as their competitors,
whereas men as a rule only have this feeling towards other men in
the same profession. Have you, reader, ever been so imprudent
as to praise an artist to another artist ? Have you ever praised a
politician to another politician of the same party ? Have you ever
praised an Egyptologist to another Egyptologist ? If you have, it is
a hundred to one that you will have produced an explosion of
jealousy. In the correspondence of Leibniz and Huyghens there
are a number of letters lamenting the supposed fact that Newton
had become insane. 'Is it not sad,' they write to each other, 'that
the incomparable genius of Mr Newton should have become
overclouded by the loss of reason ?' And these two eminent men,
in one letter after another, wept crocodile tears with obvious
relish. As a matter of fact, the event which they were hypocritically
lamenting had not taken place, though a few examples of eccentric
behaviour had given rise to the rumour.

Of all the characteristics of ordinary human nature envy is the
most unfortunate; not only does the envious person wish to inflict
misfortune and do so whenever he can with impunity, but he is
also himself rendered unhappy by envy. Instead of deriving
pleasure from what he has, he derives pain from what others have.
If he can, he deprives others of their advantages, which to him is as
desirable as it would be to secure the same advantages himself. If

this passion is allowed to run riot it becomes fatal to all excellence, and even to the most useful exercise of exceptional skill. Why should a medical man go to see his patients in a car when the labourer has to walk to his work? Why should the scientific investigator be allowed to spend his time in a warm room when others have to face the inclemency of the elements? Why should a man who possesses some rare talent of great importance to the world be saved from the drudgery of his own housework? To such questions envy finds no answer. Fortunately, however, there is in human nature a compensating passion, namely that of admiration. Whoever wishes to increase human happiness must wish to increase admiration and to diminish envy.

What cure is there for envy? For the saint there is the cure of selflessness, though even in the case of saints envy of other saints is by no means impossible. I doubt whether St Simeon Stylites would have been wholly pleased if he had learnt of some other saint who had stood even longer on an even narrower pillar. But, leaving saints out of account, the only cure for envy in the case of ordinary men and women is happiness, and the difficulty is that envy is itself a terrible obstacle to happiness. I think envy is immensely promoted by misfortunes in childhood. The child who finds a brother or sister preferred before himself acquires the habit of envy, and when he goes out into the world looks for injustices of which he is the victim, perceives them at once if they occur, and imagines them if they do not. Such a man is inevitably unhappy, and becomes a nuisance to his friends, who cannot be always remembering to avoid imaginary slights. Having begun by believing that no one likes him, he at last by his behaviour makes his belief true. Another misfortune in childhood which has the same result is to have parents without much parental feeling. Without having an unduly favoured brother or sister, a child may perceive that the children in other families are more loved by their mother and father than he is. This will cause him to hate the other children and his own parents, and when he grows up he will feel himself an Ishmael. Some kinds of happiness are everyone's natural birthright, and to be deprived of them is almost inevitably to become warped and embittered.

But the envious man may say: 'What is the good of telling me that the cure for envy is happiness? I cannot find happiness while I continue to feel envy, and you tell me that I cannot cease to be envious until I find happiness.' But real life is never so logical as this. Merely to realize the causes of one's own envious feelings is to take a long step towards curing them. The habit of thinking in terms of comparisons is a fatal one. When anything pleasant occurs it should be enjoyed to the full, without stopping to think that it is not so pleasant as something else that may possibly be happening to someone else. 'Yes,' says the envious man, 'this is a sunny day, and it is springtime, and the birds are singing, and the flowers are in bloom, but I understand that the springtime in Sicily is a thousand times more beautiful, that the birds sing more exquisitely in the groves of Helicon, and that the rose of Sharon is more lovely than any in my garden.' And as he thinks these thoughts the sun is dimmed, and the birds' song becomes a meaningless twitter, and the flowers seem not worth a moment's regard. All the other joys of life he treats in the same way. 'Yes,' he will say to himself, 'the lady of my heart is lovely, I love her and she loves me, but how much more exquisite must have been the Queen of Sheba! Ah, if I had but had Solomon's opportunities!' All such comparisons are pointless and foolish; whether the Queen of Sheba or our next-door neighbour be the cause of discontent, either is equally futile. With the wise man, what he has does not cease to be enjoyable because someone else has something else. Envy, in fact, is one form of a vice, partly moral, partly intellectual, which consists in seeing things never in themselves, but only in their relations. I am earning, let us say, a salary sufficient for my needs. I should be content, but I hear that someone else whom I believe to be in no way my superior is earning a salary twice as great as mine. Instantly, if I am of an envious disposition, the satisfactions to be derived from what I have grow dim, and I begin to be eaten up with a sense of injustice. For all this the proper cure is mental discipline, the habit of not thinking profitless thoughts. After all, what is more enviable than happiness? And if I can cure myself of envy I can acquire happiness and become enviable. The man who has double my salary is doubtless tortured by the thought that someone else in turn has twice as much as he has, and so it goes on. If you desire glory, you may envy Napoleon.

But Napoleon envied Caesar, Caesar envied Alexander, and Alexander, I daresay, envied Hercules, who never existed. You cannot, therefore, get away from envy by means of success alone, for there will always be in history or legend some person even more successful than you are. You can get away from envy by enjoying the pleasures that come your way, by doing the work that you have to do, and by avoiding comparisons with those whom you imagine, perhaps quite falsely, to be more fortunate than yourself.

Unnecessary modesty has a great deal to do with envy. Modesty is considered a virtue, but for my part I am very doubtful whether, in its more extreme forms, it deserves to be so regarded. Modest people need a great deal of reassuring, and often do not dare to attempt tasks which they are quite capable of performing. Modest people believe themselves to be outshone by those with whom they habitually associate. They are therefore particularly prone to envy, and, through envy, to unhappiness and illwill. For my part, I think there is much to be said for bringing up a boy to think himself a fine fellow. I do not believe that any peacock envies another peacock his tail, because every peacock is persuaded that his own tail is the finest in the world. The consequence of this is that peacocks are peaceable birds. Imagine how unhappy the life of a peacock would be if he had been taught that it is wicked to have a good opinion of oneself. Whenever he saw another peacock spreading out his tail, he would say to himself: 'I must not imagine that my tail is better than that, for that would be conceited, but oh, how I wish it were! That odious bird is so convinced of his own magnificence! Shall I pull out some of his feathers? And then perhaps I need no longer fear comparison with him.' Or perhaps he would lay a trap for him, and prove that he was a wicked peacock who had been guilty of unpeacockly behaviour, and he would denounce him to the assembly of the leaders. Gradually he would establish the principle that peacocks with specially fine tails are almost always wicked, and that the wise ruler in the peacock kingdom would seek out the humble bird with only a few draggled tail feathers. Having got this principle accepted, he would get all the finest birds put to death, and in the end a really splendid tail will become only a dim memory of the past. Such is the victory of envy masquerading as morality. But where every peacock thinks himself more splendid than any of the others, there is no need for all this repression. Each peacock expects to win the first prize in the competition, and each, because he values his own peahen, believes that he has done so.

Envy is, of course, closely connected with competition. We do not envy a good fortune which we conceive as quite hopelessly out of our reach. In an age when the social hierarchy is fixed, the lowest classes do not envy the upper classes so long as the division between rich and poor is thought to be ordained by God. Beggars do not envy millionaires, though of course they will envy other beggars who are more successful. The instability of social status in the modern world, and the equalitarian doctrine of democracy and socialism, have greatly extended the range of envy. For the moment this is an evil, but it is an evil which must be endured in order to arrive at a more just social system. As soon as inequalities are thought about rationally they are seen to be unjust unless they rest upon some superiority of merit. And as soon as they are seen to be unjust, there is no remedy for the resulting envy except the removal of the injustice. Our age is therefore one in which envy plays a peculiarly large part. The poor envy the rich, the poorer nations envy the richer nations, women envy men, virtuous women envy those who, though not virtuous, remain unpunished. While it is true that envy is the chief motive force leading to justice as between different classes, different nations, and different sexes, it is at the same time true that the kind of justice to be expected as a result of envy is likely to be the worst possible kind, namely that which consists rather in diminishing the pleasures of the fortunate than in increasing those of the unfortunate. Passions which work havoc in private life work havoc in public life also. It is not to be supposed that out of something as evil as envy good results will flow. Those, therefore, who from idealistic reasons desire profound changes in our social system, and a great increase of social justice, must hope that other forces than envy will be instrumental in bringing the changes about.

All bad things are interconnected, and any one of them is liable to be the cause of any other; more particularly fatigue is a very frequent cause of envy. When a man feels inadequate to the work he has to do, he feels a general discontent which is exceedingly liable to take the form of envy towards those whose work is less exacting. One of the ways of diminishing envy, therefore, is to diminish fatigue. But by far the most important thing is to secure a life which is satisfying to instinct. Much envy that seems purely professional really has a sexual source. A man who is happy in his marriage and his children is not likely to feel much envy of other men because of their greater wealth or success, so long as he has enough to bring up his children in what he feels to be the right way. The essentials of human happiness are simple, so simple that sophisticated people cannot bring themselves to admit what it is they really lack. The women we spoke of earlier who look with envy on every well-dressed woman are, one may be sure, not happy in their instinctive life. Instinctive happiness is rare in the English-speaking world, especially among women. Civilization in this respect appears to have gone astray. If there is to be less envy, means must be found for remedying this state of affairs, and if no such means are found our civilization is in danger of going down to destruction in an orgy of hatred. In old days people only envied their neighbours, because they knew little about anyone else. Now through education and the Press they know much in an abstract way about large classes of mankind of whom no single individual is among their acquaintance. Through the movies they think they know how the rich live, through the newspapers they know much of the wickedness of foreign nations, through propaganda they know of the nefarious practices of all whose skin has a pigmentation different from their own. Yellows hate whites, whites hate blacks, and so on. All this hatred, you may say, is stirred up by propaganda, but this is a somewhat shallow explanation. Why is propaganda so much more successful when it stirs up hatred than when it tries to stir up friendly feeling? The reason is clearly that the human heart as modern civilization has made it is more prone to hatred than to friendship. And it is prone to hatred because it is dissatisfied, because it feels deeply, perhaps even unconsciously, that it has somehow missed the meaning of life, that perhaps others, but not we ourselves, have secured the good things which nature offers for man's enjoyment. The positive sum of pleasures in a modern man's life is undoubtedly greater than was to be found in more primitive communities, but the consciousness of what might be has increased even more. Whenever you happen to take your children to the Zoo you may observe in the eyes of the apes, when they are not performing gymnastic feats or cracking nuts, a strange strained sadness. One can almost imagine that they feel they ought to become men, but cannot discover the secret of how to do it. On the road of evolution they have lost their way; their cousins marched on and they were left behind. Something of the same strain and anguish seems to have entered the soul of civilized man. He knows there is something better than himself almost within his grasp, yet he does not know where to seek it or how to find it. In despair he rages against his fellow man, who is equally lost and equally unhappy. We have reached a stage in evolution which is not the final stage. We must pass through it quickly, for if we do not, most of us will perish by the way, and the others will be lost in a forest of doubt and fear. Envy therefore, evil as it is, and terrible as are its effects, is not wholly of the devil. It is in part the expression of an heroic pain, the pain of those who walk through the night blindly, perhaps to a better resting-place, perhaps only to death and destruction. To find the right road out of this despair civilized man must enlarge his heart as he has enlarged his mind. He must learn to transcend self, and in so doing to acquire the freedom of the Universe.

CHAPTER VII

The Sense of Sin

CONCERNING the sense of sin we have already in Chapter I had occasion to say something, but we must now go into it more fully, since it is one of the most important of the underlying psychological causes of unhappiness in adult life.

There is a traditional religious psychology of sin which no modern psychologist can accept. It was supposed, especially by Protestants, that conscience reveals to every man when an act to which he is tempted is sinful, and that after committing such an act he may experience either of two painful feelings, one called remorse, in which there is no merit, and the other called repentance, which is capable of wiping out his guilt. In Protestant countries even many of those who lost their faith continued for a time to accept with greater or smaller modifications the orthodox view of sin. In our own day, partly owing to psycho-analysis, we have the opposite state of affairs: not only do the unorthodox reject the old doctrine of sin, but many of those who still consider themselves orthodox do so likewise. Conscience has ceased to be something mysterious which, because it was mysterious, could be regarded as the voice of God. We know that conscience enjoins different acts in different parts of the world, and that broadly speaking it is everywhere in agreement with tribal custom. What, then, is really happening when a man's conscience pricks him?

The word 'conscience' covers, as a matter of fact, several different feelings; the simplest of these is the fear of being found out. You, reader, have, I am sure, lived a completely blameless life, but if you will ask someone who has at some time acted in a manner for which he would be punished if it became known, you will find that, when discovery seemed imminent, the person in question repented of his crime. I do not say that this would apply to the professional thief who expects a certain amount of prison as a trade risk, but it applies to what may be called the respectable offender, such as the Bank Manager who has embezzled in a moment of stress, or the clergyman who has been tempted by passion into some sensual irregularity. Such men can forget their crime when there seems little chance of detection, but when they are found out, or in grave danger of being so, they wish they had been more virtuous, and this wish may give them a lively sense of the enormity of their sin. Closely allied with this feeling is the fear of becoming an outcast from the herd. A man who cheats at cards or fails to pay his debts of honour has nothing within himself by which to stand up against the disapproval of the herd when he is found out. In this he is unlike the religious innovator, the anarchist, and the revolutionary, who all feel that, whatever may be their fate in the present, the future is with them and will honour them as much as they are execrated in the present. These men, in spite of the hostility of the herd, do not feel sinful, but the man who entirely accepts the morality of the herd while acting against it suffers great unhappiness when he loses caste, and the fear of this disaster, or the pain of it when it has happened, may easily cause him to regard his acts themselves as sinful.

But the sense of sin in its most important forms is something which goes deeper. It is something which has its roots in the unconscious, and does not appear in consciousness as fear of other people's disapproval. In consciousness certain kinds of acts are labelled Sin for no reason visible to introspection. When a man commits these acts he feels uncomfortable without quite knowing why. He wishes he were the kind of man who could abstain from what he believes to be sin. He gives moral admiration only to those whom he believes to be pure in heart. He recognizes with a greater or less degree of regret that it is not for him to be a saint; indeed, his conception of saintship is probably one which it is nearly impossible to carry out in an ordinary everyday life. Consequently he goes through life with a sense of guilt, feeling that the best is not for him, and that his highest moments are those of maudlin penitence.

The source of all this in practically every case is the moral teaching which the man received before he was six years old at the hands of his mother or his nurse. He learned before that age that it is wicked to swear, and not quite nice to use any but the most ladylike language, that only bad men drink, and that tobacco is incompatible with the highest virtue. He learned that one should never tell a lie. And above all he learned that any interest in the sexual parts is an abomination. He knew these to be the view of his mother, and believed them to be those of his Creator. To be affectionately treated by his mother, or, if she was neglectful, by his nurse, was the greatest pleasure of his life, and was only obtainable when he had not been known to sin against the moral code. He therefore came to associate something vaguely awful with any conduct of which his mother or nurse would disapprove. Gradually as he grew older he forgot where his moral code had come from and what had originally been the penalty for disobeying it, but he did not throw off the moral code or cease to feel that something dreadful was liable to happen to him if he infringed it.

Now very large parts of this infantile moral teaching are devoid of all rational foundation and such as cannot be applied to the ordinary behaviour of ordinary men. A man who uses what is called 'bad language', for example, is not from a rational point of view any worse than a man who does not. Nevertheless, practically everybody in trying to imagine a saint would consider abstinence from swearing as essential. Considered in the light of reason this is simply silly. The same applies to alcohol and tobacco. With regard to alcohol the feeling does not exist in Southern countries, and indeed there is an element of impiety about it, since it is known that Our Lord and the Apostles drank wine. With regard to tobacco it is easier to maintain a negative position since all the greatest saints lived before its use was known. But here also no rational argument is possible. The view that no saint would smoke is based in the last analysis upon the view that no saint would do anything solely because it gave him pleasure. This ascetic element in ordinary morality has become almost unconscious but it operates in all kinds of ways that make our moral code irrational. In a rational ethic it will be held laudable to give pleasure to anyone, even to oneself, provided there is no counterbalancing pain to oneself or to others. The ideally virtuous man, if we had got rid of asceticism, would be the man who permits the enjoyment of all good things whenever there is no evil consequence to outweigh the enjoyment. Take again the question of lying. I do not deny that there is a great deal too much lying in the world, and that we should all be the better for an increase of truthfulness, but I do deny, as I think every rational person must, that lying is in no circumstances justified. I once in the course of a country walk saw a tired fox at the last stages of exhaustion still forcing himself to run. A few minutes afterwards I saw the hunt. They asked me if I had seen the fox, and I said I had. They asked me which way he had gone, and I lied to them. I do not think I should have been a better man if I had told the truth.

But it is above all in the realm of sex that early moral teaching does harm. If a child has been conventionally educated by somewhat stern parents or nurses, the association between sin and the sex organs is so firmly established by the time he is six years old that it is unlikely ever to be completely undone throughout the rest of his life. This feeling is, of course, reinforced by the Œdipus complex, since the woman most loved in childhood is one with whom all sexual freedoms are impossible. The result is that many adult men feel women to be degraded by sex, and cannot respect their wives unless their wives hate sexual intercourse. But the man whose wife is cold will be driven by instinct to seek instinctive satisfaction elsewhere. His instinctive satisfaction, however, even if he momentarily finds it, will be poisoned by the sense of guilt, so that he cannot be happy in any relation with a woman, whether in marriage or outside it. On the woman's side the same sort of thing happens if she has been very emphatically taught to be what is called 'pure'. She instinctively holds herself back in her sexual relations with her husband, and is afraid of deriving any pleasure from them. In the present day, however, there is very much less of this on the part of women than there was fifty years ago. I should say that at present among educated people the sex life of men is more contorted and more poisoned by the sense of sin than that of women.

There is beginning to be widespread awareness, though not of course on the part of public authorities, of the evils of traditional sex education in regard to the very young. The right rule is simple:

C

until a child is nearing the age of puberty teach him or her no sexual morality whatever, and carefully avoid instilling the idea that there is anything disgusting in the natural bodily functions. As the time approaches when it becomes necessary to give moral instruction, be sure that it is rational, and that at every point you can give good grounds for what you say. But it is not on education that I wish to speak in this book. In this book I am concerned rather with what the adult can do to minimize the evil effects of unwise education in causing an irrational sense of sin.

The problem here is the same as has confronted us in earlier chapters, namely that of compelling the unconscious to take note of the rational beliefs that govern our conscious thought. Men must not allow themselves to be swayed by their moods, believing one thing at one moment and another at another. The sense of sin is especially prominent at moments when the conscious will is weakened by fatigue, by illness, by drink, or by any other cause. What a man feels at these moments (unless caused by drink) is supposed to be a revelation from his higher self. 'The devil was sick, the devil a saint would be.' But it is absurd to suppose that moments of weakness give more insight than moments of strength. In moments of weakness it is difficult to resist infantile suggestions, but there is no reason whatsoever for regarding such suggestions as preferable to the beliefs of the adult man when in full possession of his faculties. On the contrary, what a man deliberately believes with his whole reason when he is vigorous ought to be to him the norm as to what he had better believe at all times. It is quite possible to overcome infantile suggestions of the unconscious, and even to change the contents of the unconscious, by employing the right kind of technique. Whenever you begin to feel remorse for an act which your reason tells you is not wicked, examine the causes of your feeling of remorse, and convince yourself in detail of their absurdity. Let your conscious beliefs be so vivid and emphatic that they make an impression upon your unconscious strong enough to cope with the impressions made by your nurse or your mother when you were an infant. Do not be content with an alternation between moments of rationality and moments of irrationality. Look into the irrationality closely, with a deter- mination not to respect it, and not to let it dominate you. Whenever it thrusts foolish thoughts or feelings into your consciousness, pull them up by the roots, examine them, and reject them. Do not allow yourself to remain a vacillating creature, swayed half by reason and half by infantile folly. Do not be afraid of irreverence towards the memory of those who controlled your childhood. They seemed to you then strong and wise because you were weak and foolish; now that you are neither, it is your business to examine their apparent strength and wisdom, to consider whether they deserve that reverence that from force of habit you still bestow upon them. Ask yourself seriously whether the world is the better for the moral teaching traditionally given to the young. Consider how much of unadulterated superstition goes into the make-up of the conventionally virtuous man, and reflect that, while all kinds of imaginary moral dangers were guarded against by incredibly foolish prohibitions, the real moral dangers to which an adult is exposed were practically unmentioned. What are the really harmful acts to which the average man is tempted? Sharp practice in business of the sort not punished by law, harshness towards employees, cruelty towards wife and children, malevolence towards competitors, ferocity in political conflicts—these are the really harmful sins that are common among respectable and respected citizens. By means of these sins a man spreads misery in his immediate circle and does his bit towards destroying civilization. Yet these are not the things that make him, when he is ill, regard himself as an outcast who has forfeited all claim to divine favour. These are not the things that cause him in nightmares to see visions of his mother bending reproachful glances upon him. Why is his subconscious morality thus divorced from reason? Because the ethic believed in by those who had charge of his infancy was silly; because it was not derived from any study of the individual's duty to the community; because it was made up of old scraps of irrational taboos; and because it contained within itself elements of morbidness derived from the spiritual sickness that troubled the dying Roman Empire. Our nominal morality has been formulated by priests and mentally enslaved women. It is time that men who have to take a normal part in the normal life of the world learned to rebel against this sickly nonsense.

But if the rebellion is to be successful in bringing individual happiness and in enabling a man to live consistently by one standard, not to vacillate between two, it is necessary that he should think and feel deeply about what his reason tells him. Most men, when they have thrown off superficially the superstitions of their childhood, think that there is no more to be done. They do not realize that these superstitions are still lurking underground. When a rational conviction has been arrived at, it is necessary to dwell upon it, to follow out its consequences, to search out in oneself whatever beliefs inconsistent with the new conviction might otherwise survive, and when the sense of sin grows strong, as from time to time it will, to treat it not as a revelation and a call to higher things, but as a disease and a weakness, unless of course it is caused by some act which a rational ethic would condemn. I am not suggesting that a man should be destitute of morality, I am only suggesting that he should be destitute of superstitious morality, which is a very different thing.

But even when a man has offended against his own rational code, I doubt whether a sense of sin is the best method of arriving at a better way of life. There is in the sense of sin something abject, something lacking in self-respect. No good was ever done to anyone by the loss of self-respect. The rational man will regard his own undesirable acts as he regards those of others, as acts produced by certain circumstances, and to be avoided either by a fuller realization that they are undesirable, or, where this is possible, by avoidance of the circumstances that caused them.

As a matter of fact the sense of sin, so far from being a cause of a good life, is quite the reverse. It makes a man unhappy and it makes him feel inferior. Being unhappy, he is likely to make claims upon other people which are excessive and which prevent him from enjoying happiness in personal relations. Feeling inferior, he will have a grudge against those who seem superior. He will find admiration difficult and envy easy. He will become a generally disagreeable person, and will find himself more and more solitary. An expansive and generous attitude towards other people not only gives happiness to others, but is an immense source of happiness to its possessor, since it causes him to be generally liked. But such an attitude is scarcely possible to the man haunted by a sense of sin. It is an outcome of poise and self-reliance; it demands what may be called mental integration, by which I mean that the various layers of a man's nature, conscious, subconscious, and unconscious, work together harmoniously and are not engaged in perpetual battle. To produce such harmony is possible in most cases by wise education, but where education has been unwise it is a more difficult process. It is the process which the psycho-analysts attempt, but I believe that in a very great many cases the patient can himself perform the work which in more extreme cases requires the help of the expert. Do not say: 'I have no time for such psychological labours; my life is a busy one filled with affairs, and I must leave my unconscious to its tricks.' Nothing so much diminishes not only happiness but efficiency as a personality divided against itself. The time spent in producing harmony between the different parts of one's personality is time usefully employed. I do not suggest that a man should set apart, say, an hour a day for self-examination. This is to my mind by no means the best method, since it increases self-absorption, which is part of the disease to be cured, for a harmonious personality is directed outward. What I suggest is that a man should make up his mind with emphasis as to what he rationally believes, and should never allow contrary irrational beliefs to pass unchallenged or obtain a hold over him, however brief. This is a question of reasoning with himself in those moments in which he is tempted to become infantile, but the reasoning, if it is sufficiently emphatic, may be very brief. The time involved, therefore, should be negligible.

There is in many people a dislike of rationality, and where this exists the kind of thing that I have been saying will seem irrelevant and unimportant. There is an idea that rationality, if allowed free play, will kill all the deeper emotions. This belief appears to me to be due to an entirely erroneous conception of the function of reason in human life. It is not the business of reason to generate emotions, though it may be part of its function to discover ways of preventing such emotions as are an obstacle to well-being. To find ways of minimizing hatred and envy is no doubt part of the function of a rational psychology. But it is a mistake to suppose that in minimizing these passions we shall at the same time diminish the strength of those passions which reason does not condemn. In passionate love, in parental affection, in friendship, in benevolence, in devotion to science or art, there is nothing that reason should wish to diminish. The rational man, when he feels any or all of these emotions, will be glad that he feels them and will do nothing to lessen their strength, for all these emotions are parts of the good life, the life, that is, that makes for happiness both in oneself and in others. There is nothing irrational in the passions as such, and many irrational people feel only the most trivial passions. No man need fear that by making himself rational he will make his life dull. On the contrary, since rationality consists in the main of internal harmony, the man who achieves it is freer in his contemplation of the world and in the use of his energies to achieve external purposes than is the man who is prepetually hampered by inward conflicts. Nothing is so dull as to be encased in self, nothing so exhilarating as to have attention and energy directed outwards.

Our traditional morality has been unduly self-centred, and the conception of sin is part of this unwise focusing of attention upon self. To those who have never passed through the subjective moods induced by this faulty morality, reason may be unnecessary. But to those who have once acquired the sickness, reason is necessary in effecting a cure. And perhaps the sickness is a necessary stage in mental development. I am inclined to think that the man who has passed beyond it by the help of reason has reached a higher level than the man who has never experienced either the sickness or the cure. The hatred of reason which is common in our time is very largely due to the fact that the operations of reason are not conceived in a sufficiently fundamental way. The man divided against himself looks for excitement and distraction; he loves strong passions, not for sound reasons, but because for the moment they take him outside himself and prevent the painful necessity of thought. Any passion is to him a form of intoxication, and since he cannot conceive of fundamental happiness, all relief from pain appears to him solely possible in the form of intoxication. This, however, is the symptom of a deep-seated malady. Where there is no such malady, the greatest happiness comes with the most complete possession of one's faculties. It is in the moments when the mind is most active and the fewest things are forgotten that the most intense joys are experienced. This, indeed, is one of the best touchstones of happiness. The happiness that requires intoxication of no matter what sort is a spurious and unsatisfying kind. The happiness that is genuinely satisfying is accompanied by the fullest exercise of our faculties, and the fullest realization of the world in which we live.

CHAPTER VIII

Persecution Mania

IN its more extreme forms persecution mania is a recognized form of insanity. Some people imagine that others wish to kill them, or imprison them, or to do them some other grave injury. Often the wish to protect themselves against imaginary persecutors leads them into acts of violence which make it necessary to restrain their liberty. This, like many other forms of insanity, is only an exaggeration of a tendency not at all uncommon among people who count as normal. I do not propose to discuss the extreme forms, which are a matter for a psychiatrist. It is the milder forms that I wish to consider, because they are a very frequent cause of unhappiness, and because, not having gone so far as to produce definite insanity, they are still capable of being dealt with by the patient himself, provided he can be induced to diagnose his trouble rightly and to see that its origin lies within himself and not in the supposed hostility or unkindness of others.

We are all familiar with the type of person, man or woman, who, according to his own account, is perpetually the victim of ingratitude, unkindness, and treachery. People of this kind are often extraordinarily plausible, and secure warm sympathy from those who have not known them long. There is, as a rule, nothing inherently improbable about each separate story that they relate. The kind of ill-treatment of which they complain does undoubtedly sometimes occur. What in the end rouses the hearer's suspicions is the multiplicity of villains whom it has been the sufferer's ill-fortune to meet with. In accordance with the doctrine of probability, different people living in a given society are likely in the course of their lives to meet with about the same amount of bad treatment. If one person in a given set receives, according to his own account, universal ill-treatment, the likelihood is that the cause lies in himself, and that he either imagines injuries from which in fact he has not suffered, or unconsciously behaves in such a way as to arouse uncontrollable irritation. Experienced people therefore become suspicious of those who by their own account are invariably ill-treated by the world; they tend, by their lack of sympathy, to confirm these unfortunate people in the view that everyone is against them. The trouble, in fact, is a difficult one to deal with, since it is inflamed alike by sympathy and by lack of sympathy. The person inclined to persecution mania, when he finds a hard-luck story believed, will embellish it until he reaches the frontier of credibility; when, on the other hand, he finds it disbelieved, he has merely another example of the peculiar hard-heartedness of mankind towards himself. The disease is one that can be dealt with by understanding, and this understanding must be conveyed to the patient if it is to serve its purpose. My purpose in this chapter is to suggest some general reflections by means of which each individual can detect in himself the elements of persecution mania (from which almost everybody suffers in a greater or less degree), and, having detected them, can eliminate them. This is an important part of the conquest of happiness, since it is quite impossible to be happy if we feel that everybody ill-treats us.

One of the most universal forms of irrationality is the attitude taken by practically everybody towards malicious gossip. Very few people can resist saying malicious things about their acquaintances, and even on occasion about their friends; yet when people hear that anything has been said against themselves, they are filled with indignant amazement. It has apparently never occurred to them that, just as they gossip about everyone else, so everyone else gossips about them. This is a mild form of the attitude which, when exaggerated, leads on to persecution mania. We expect everybody else to feel towards us that tender love and that profound respect which we feel towards ourselves. It does not occur to us that we cannot expect others to think better of us than we think of them and the reason this does not occur to us is that our own merits are great and obvious, whereas those of others, if they exist at all, are only visible to a very charitable eye. When you hear that so-and-so has said something horrid about you, you remember the ninety-nine times when you have refrained from uttering the most just and well-deserved criticism of him, and forget the hundredth time when in an unguarded moment you have declared what you believe to be the truth about him. Is this the reward, you feel, for all your long forbearance? Yet from his point of view your conduct appears exactly what his appears to you; he knows nothing of the times when you have not spoken, he knows only of the hundredth time when you did speak. If we were all given by magic the power to read each other's thoughts I suppose the first effect would be that almost all friendships would be dissolved; the second effect, however, might be excellent, for a world without any friends would be felt to be intolerable, and wc should learn to like each other without needing a veil of illusion to conceal from ourselves that we did not think each other absolutely perfect. We know that our friends have their faults, and yet are on the whole agreeable people whom we like. We find it, however, intolerable that they should have the same attitude towards us. We expect them to think that, unlike the rest of mankind, we have no faults. When we are compelled to admit that we have faults, we take this obvious fact far too seriously. Nobody should expect to be perfect, or be unduly troubled by the fact that he is not.

Persecution mania is always rooted in a too exaggerated conception of our own merits. I am, we will say, a playwright; to every unbiased person it must be obvious that I am the most brilliant playwright of the age. Nevertheless, for some reason, my plays are seldom performed, and when they are, they are not successful. What is the explanation of this strange state of affairs? Obviously that managers, actors, and critics have combined against me for one reason or another. The reason, of course, is highly creditable to myself: I have refused to kow-tow to the great ones of the theatrical world; I have not flattered the critics; my plays contain home truths which are unbearable to those whom they hit. And so my transcendent merit languishes unrecognized.

Then there is the inventor who has never been able to get anyone to examine the merits of his invention; manufacturers are set in their ways and will not consider any innovation, while the few who are progressive keep inventors of their own, who succeed in warding off the intrusions of unauthorized genius; the learned societies, strangely enough, lose one's manuscripts or return them unread; individuals to whom one appeals are unaccountably 'unresponsive. How is such a state of affairs to be explained? Obviously there is a close corporation of men who wish to divide among themselves the plums to be obtained by means of invention; the man who does not belong to this close corporation will not be listened to.

Then there is the man who has a genuine grievance founded upon actual fact, but who generalizes in the light of his experience and arrives at the conclusion that his own misfortune affords the key to the universe; he discovers, let us say, some scandal about the Secret Service which it is to the interest of the Government to keep dark. He can obtain hardly any publicity for his discovery, and the most apparently high-minded men refuse to lift a finger to remedy the evil which fills him with indignation. So far the facts are as he says they are. But his rebuffs have made such an impression upon him that he believes all powerful men to be occupied wholly and solely in covering up the crimes to which they owe their power. Cases of this kind are particularly obstinate, owing to the partial truth of their outlook; the thing that has touched them personally has made, as is natural, more impression upon them than the much larger number of matters of which they have had no direct experience. This gives them a wrong sense of proportion, and causes them to attach undue importance to facts which are perhaps exceptional rather then typical.

Another not uncommon victim of persecution mania is a certain type of philanthropist who is always doing good to people against their will, and is amazed and horrified that they display no gratitude. Our motives in doing good are seldom as pure as we imagine them to be. Love of power is insidious; it has many disguises, and is often the source of the pleasure we derive from doing what we believe to be good to other people. Not infrequently, yet another element enters in. 'Doing good' to people generally consists in depriving them of some pleasure: drink, or gambling, or idleness, or what not. In this case there is an element which is typical of much social morality, namely envy of those who are in a position to commit sins from which we have to abstain if we are to retain the respect of our friends. Those who vote, let us say, for a law against cigarette smoking (such laws exist, or existed, in several American States) are obviously non-smokers to whom the pleasure which others derive from tobacco is a source of pain. If they expect those who were previously cigarette fiends to come in a deputation and thank them for emancipation from this odious vice, it is possible that they may be disappointed. They may then begin to reflect that they have given their lives for the public good, and that those who have most reason for thanking them for their beneficent activities appear to be the least aware of any occasion for gratitude.

One used to find the same kind of attitude on the part of mistresses towards domestic servants whose morals they safeguarded. But in these days the servant problem has become so acute that this form of kindness to maids has become less common.

In the higher walks of politics the same sort of thing occurs. The statesman who has gradually concentrated all power within himself in order that he may be able to carry out the high and noble aims which have led him to eschew comfort and enter the arena of public life, is amazed at the ingratitude of the people when they turn against him. It never occurs to him that his work may have had anything but a public motive, or that the pleasure of controlling affairs may have in any degree inspired his activities. The phrases which are customary on the platform and in the Party Press have gradually come to him to seem to express truths, and he mistakes the rhetoric of partisanship for a genuine analysis of motives. Disgusted and disillusioned, he retires from the world after the world has retired from him, and regrets that he ever attempted so thankless a task as the pursuit of the public good.

These illustrations suggest four general maxims, which will prove an adequate preventive of persecution mania if their truth is sufficiently realized. The first is: remember that your motives are not always as altruistic as they seem to yourself. The second is: don't over-estimate your own merits. The third is: don't expect others to take as much interest in you as you do yourself. And the fourth is: don't imagine that most people give enough thought to you to have any special desire to persecute you. I shall say a few words about each of these maxims in turn.

Suspicion of one's own motives is especially necessary for the philanthropist and the executive; such people have a vision of how the world, or some part of it, should be, and they feel, sometimes rightly, sometimes wrongly, that in realizing their vision they will be conferring a boon upon mankind or some section of it. They do not, however, adequately realize that the individuals affected by their operations have each an equal right to his own view as to the sort of world he wants. A man of the executive type is quite sure that his vision is right, and that any contrary one is wrong. But his subjective certainty affords no proof that he is objectively right. Moreover, his belief is very often only a camouflage for the pleasure that he derives from contemplating changes of which he is the cause. And in addition to love of power there is another motive, namely vanity, which operates strongly in such cases. The high-minded idealist who stands for Parliament—on this matter I speak from experience—is astonished by the cynicism of the electorate which assumes that he only desires the glory of writing the letters 'M.P.' after his name. When the contest is over and he has time to think, it occurs to him that perhaps after all the cynical electors were in the right. Idealism causes simple motives to wear strange disguises, and therefore some dash of realistic cynicism does not come amiss in our public men. Conventional morality inculcates a degree of altruism of which human nature is scarcely capable, and those who pride themselves upon their virtue often imagine that they attain this unattainable ideal. The immense majority of even the noblest persons' actions have self-regarding motives, nor is this to be regretted, since, if it were otherwise, the human race could not survive. A man who spent his time seeing that others were fed and forgot to feed himself would perish. He may, of course, take nourishment solely in order to provide himself with the necessary strength to plunge again into the battle against evil, but it is doubtful whether food eaten with this motive could be adequately digested, since the flow of saliva would be insufficiently stimulated. It is better therefore that a man should eat because he enjoys his food than that the time he spends at his meals should be solely inspired by a desire for the public good.

And what applies to eating applies to everything else. Whatever is to be done can only be done adequately by the help of a certain zest, and zest is difficult without some self-regarding motive. I should include among self-regarding motives, from this point of view, those that concern persons biologically connected with oneself, such as the impulse to the defence of wife and children against enemies. This degree of altruism is part of normal human nature, but the degree inculcated in conventional ethics is not, and is very rarely attained genuinely. People who wish to have a high opinion of their own moral excellence have therefore to persuade themselves that they have achieved a degree of unselfishness that it is very unlikely that they have achieved, and hence the endeavour after saintliness comes to be connected with self-deception of a kind that easily leads on to persecution mania.

The second of our four maxims, to the effect that it is unwise to over-estimate your own merits, is covered, so far as morals are concerned, by what we have already said. But merits other than moral should equally not be over-estimated. The playwright whose plays never succeed should consider calmly the hypothesis that they are bad plays; he should not reject this out of hand as obviously untenable. If he finds that it fits the facts, he should, as an inductive philosopher, adopt it. It is true that there are in history cases of unrecognized merit, but they are far less numerous than the cases of recognized demerit. If a man is a genius whom the age will not recognize, he is quite right to persist in his course in spite of lack of recognition. If, on the other hand, he is an un-talented person puffed up with vanity, he will do well not to persist. There is no way of knowing to which of these two categories one belongs if one is afflicted with the impulse to produce unrecognized masterpieces. If you belong to the one category, your persistence is heroic; if to the other, ludicrous. When you have been dead a hundred years, it will be possible to guess to which category you belonged. In the meantime, there is a test, not perhaps infallible, but yet of considerable value, which you may apply yourself if you suspect that you are a genius while your friends suspect that you are not. The test is this: do you produce because you feel an urgent compulsion to express certain ideas or feelings, or are you actuated by the desire for applause? In the genuine artist the desire for applause, while it usually exists strongly, is secondary, in the sense that the artist wishes to produce a certain kind of work, and hopes that that work may be applauded, but will not alter his style even if no applause is forthcoming. The man, on the other hand, to whom the desire for applause is the primary motive, has no force within himself urging him to a particular kind of expression, and could therefore just as well do work of some wholly different kind. Such a man, if he fails to win applause by his art, had better give it up. And, speaking more generally, whatever your line in life may be, if you find that others do not rate your abilities as highly as you do yourself, do not be too sure that it is they who are mistaken. If you allow yourself to think this, you may easily fall into the belief that there is a conspiracy to prevent the recognition of your merit, and this belief is pretty sure to be the source of an unhappy life. To recognize that your merit is not so great as you had hoped may be more painful for a moment, but it is a pain which has an end, beyond which a happy life again becomes possible.

Our third maxim was not to expect too much of others. It used to be customary for invalid ladies to expect at least one of their daughters to sacrifice themselves completely in performing the duties of a nurse, even to the extent of forgoing marriage. This is to expect of another a degree of altruism which is contrary to reason, since the loss to the altruist is greater than the gain to the egoist. In all your dealings with other people, especially with those who are nearest and dearest, it is important and not always easy to remember that they see life from their own angle and as it touches their own ego, not from your angle and as it touches yours. No person should be expected to distort the main lines of his life for the sake of another individual. On occasion there may exist such a strong affection that even the greatest sacrifices become natural, but if they are not natural they should not be made, and no person should be held blameworthy for not making them. Very often the conduct that people complain of in others is not more than the healthy reaction of natural egoism against the grasping rapacity of a person whose ego extends beyond its proper limits.

The fourth maxim that we mentioned consists of realizing that other people spend less time in thinking about you than you do yourself. The insane victim of persecution mania imagines that all sorts of people, who, in fact, have their own avocations and interests, are occupied morning, noon, and night in an endeavour to work a mischief to the poor lunatic. In like manner, the comparatively sane victim of persecution mania sees in all kinds of actions a reference to himself which does not, in fact, exist. This idea, of course, is flattering to his vanity. If he were a great enough man, it might be true. The actions of the British Government for many years were mainly concerned to thwart Napoleon. But when a person of no special importance imagines that others are personally thinking about him, he is on the road towards insanity. You make a speech, let us say, at some public dinner. Photographs of some of the other speakers appear in the picture papers, but there is no picture of you. How is this to be accounted for? Obviously not because the other speakers were considered more important; it must be because the editors of the papers had given orders that you were to be ignored. And why should they have given such orders? Obviously because they feared you on account of your great importance. In this way the omission of your picture is transformed from a slight into a subtle compliment. But self-deception of this kind cannot lead to any solid happiness. In the back of your mind you will know that the facts are otherwise, and in order to conceal this from yourself as far as possible, you will have to invent more and more fantastic hypotheses. The strain of trying to believe these will, in the end, become very great. And since, moreover, they involve the belief that you are the object of widespread hostility, they will only safeguard your self-esteem by inflicting the very painful feeling that you are at odds with the world. No satisfaction based upon self-deception is solid, and, however unpleasant the truth may be, it is better to face it once for all, to get used to it, and to proceed to build your life in accordance with it.

CHAPTER IX

Fear of Public Opinion

VERY few people can be happy unless on the whole their way of life and their outlook on the world is approved by those with whom they have social relations, and more especially by those with whom they live. It is a peculiarity of modern communities that they are divided into sets which differ profoundly in their morals and in their beliefs. This state of affairs began with the Reformation, or perhaps one should say with the Renaissance, and has grown more pronounced ever since. There were Protestants and Catholics, who differed not only in theology but on many more practical matters. There were aristocrats who permitted various kinds of action that were not tolerated among the bourgeoisie. Then there came to be latitudinarians and free-thinkers who did not recognize the duties of religious observance. In our own day throughout the Continent of Europe there is a profound division between socialists and others, which covers not only politics but almost every department of life. In English-speaking countries the divisions are very numerous. In some sets art is admired, while in others it is thought to be of the devil, at any rate if it is modern. In some sets devotion to the Empire is the supreme virtue, in others it is considered a vice, and yet in others a form of stupidity. Conventional people consider adultery one of the worst of crimes, but large sections of the population regard it as excusable if not positively laudable. Among Catholics divorce is totally forbidden, while most non-Catholics accept it as a necessary alleviation of matrimony.

Owing to all these differences of outlook a person of given tastes and convictions may find himself practically an outcast while he lives in one set, although in another set he would be accepted as an entirely ordinary human being. A very great deal of unhappiness, especially among the young, arises in this way. A young man or young woman somehow catches ideas that are in the air, but finds that these ideas are anathema in the particular milieu in which he or she lives. It easily seems to the young as if the only milieu with which they are acquainted were representative of the whole world. They can scarcely believe that in another place or another set the views which they dare not avow for fear of being thought utterly perverse would be accepted as the ordinary commonplaces of the age. Thus through ignorance of the world a great deal of unnecessary misery is endured, sometimes only in youth, but not infrequently throughout life. This isolation is not only a source of pain, it also causes a great dissipation of energy in the unnecessary task of maintaining mental independence against hostile surroundings, and in ninety-nine cases out of a hundred produces a certain timidity in following out ideas to their logical conclusions. The Brontë sisters never met any congenial people until after their books had been published. This did not affect Emily, who was heroic and in the grand manner, but it certainly did affect Charlotte, whose outlook, in spite of her talents, remained always to a large extent that of a governess. Blake, like Emily Brontë, lived in extreme mental isolation, but like her was great enough to overcome its bad effects, since he never doubted that he was right and his critics wrong. His attitude towards public opinion is expressed in the lines:

> The only man that e'er I knew
> Who did not make me almost spew
> Was Fuseli: he was both Turk and Jew.
> And so, dear Christian friends, how do you do?

But there are not many who have this degree of force in their inner life. To almost everybody sympathetic surroundings are necessary to happiness. To the majority, of course, the surroundings in which they happen to find themselves are sympathetic. They imbibe current prejudices in youth, and instinctively adapt themselves to the beliefs and customs which they find in existence around them. But to a large minority which includes practically all who have any intellectual or artistic merit, this attitude of acquiescence is impossible. A person born, let us say, in some small country town finds himself from early youth surrounded by hostility to everything that is necessary for mental excellence. If he wishes to read serious books, other boys despise him, and teachers tell him that such works are unsettling. If he cares for art, his contemporaries think him unmanly, and his elders think him immoral. If he desires any career, however respectable, which has not been common in the circle to which he belongs, he is told that he is setting himself up, and that what was good enough for his father ought to be good enough for him. If he shows any tendency to criticize his parents' religious tenets or political affiliations, he is likely to find himself in serious trouble. For all these reasons, to most young men and young women of exceptional merit adolescence is a time of great unhappiness. To their more ordinary companions it may be a time of gaiety and enjoyment, but for themselves they want something more serious, which they can find neither among their elders nor among their contemporaries in the particular social setting in which chance has caused them to be born.

When such young people go to a University they probably discover congenial souls and enjoy a few years of great happiness. If they are fortunate, they may succeed, on leaving the University, in obtaining some kind of work that gives them still the possibility of choosing congenial companions; an intelligent man who live in a city as large as London or New York can generally find some congenial set in which it is not necessary to practise any constraint or hypocrisy. But if his work obliges him to live in some smaller place, and more particularly if it necessitates retention of the respect of ordinary people, as is the case, for example, with a doctor or a lawyer, he may find himself throughout his whole life practically compelled to conceal his real tastes and convictions from most of the people that he meets in the course of his day. This is especially true in America because of the vastness of the country. In the most unlikely places, north, south, east, and west, one finds lonely individuals who know from books that there are places where they would not be lonely, but who have no chance to live in such places, and only the rarest opportunity of congenial conversation. Real happiness in such circumstances is impossible to those who are built on a less magnificent scale than Blake and Emily Brontë. If it is to become possible, some way must be found by which the tyranny of public opinion can be either lessened or evaded, and by which members of the intelligent minority can come to know each other and enjoy each other's society.

In a good many cases unnecessary timidity makes the trouble worse than it need be. Public opinion is always more tyrannical towards those who obviously fear it than towards those who feel indifferent to it. A dog will bark more loudly and bite more readily when people are afraid of him than when they treat him with contempt, and the human herd has something of this same characteristic. If you show that you are afraid of them, you give promise of good hunting, whereas if you show indifference, they begin to doubt their own power and therefore tend to let you alone. I am not, of course, thinking of extreme forms of defiance. If you hold in Kensington the views that are conventional in Russia, or in Russia the views that are conventional in Kensington, you must accept the consequences. I am thinking, not of such extremes but of much milder lapses from conventionality, such as failure to dress correctly or to belong to some Church or to abstain from reading intelligent books. Such lapses, if they are done with gaiety and insouciance, not defiantly but spontaneously, will come to be tolerated even in the most conventional society. Gradually it may become possible to acquire the position of licensed lunatic, to whom things are permitted which in another man would be thought unforgivable. This is largely a matter of a certain kind of good nature and friendliness. Conventional people are roused to fury by departures from convention, largely because they regard such departures as a criticism of themselves. They will pardon much unconventionality in a man who has enough jollity and friendliness to make it clear, even to the stupidest, that he is not engaged in criticizing them.

This method of escaping censure is, however, impossible to many of those whose tastes or opinions cause them to be out of sympathy with the herd. Their lack of sympathy makes them uncomfortable and causes them to have a pugnacious attitude, even if outwardly they conform or manage to avoid any sharp issue. People who are not in harmony with the conventions of their own set tend therefore to be prickly and uncomfortable and lacking in expansive good humour. These same people, transported into another set where their outlook is not thought strange, will seem to change their character entirely. From being serious, shy and retiring they may become gay and self-confident; from being angular they may become smooth and easy; from being self-centred they may become sociable and extravert.

Wherever possible, therefore, young people who find themselves out of harmony with their surroundings should endeavour in the choice of a profession to select some career which will give them a chance of congenial companionship, even if this should entail a considerable loss of income. Often they hardly know that this is possible, since their knowledge of the world is very limited, and they may easily imagine that the prejudices to which they have become accustomed at home are world wide. This is a matter in which older men should be able to give much assistance to the young, since a considerable experience of mankind is essential.

It is customary in these days of psycho-analysis to assume that, when any young person is out of harmony with his environment, the cause must lie in some psychological disorder. This is to my mind a complete mistake. Suppose, for example, that a young person has parents who believe the doctrine of evolution to be wicked. Nothing except intelligence is required in such a case to cause him to be out of sympathy with them. To be out of harmony with one's surroundings is, of course, a misfortune, but it is not always a misfortune to be avoided at all costs. Where the environment is stupid or prejudiced or cruel, it is a sign of merit to be out of harmony with it. And to some degree these characteristics exist in almost every environment. Galileo and Kepler had 'dangerous thoughts' (as they are called in Japan), and so have the most intelligent men of our own day. It is not desirable that the social sense should be so strongly developed as to cause such men to fear the social hostility which their opinions may provoke. What is desirable is to find ways of making this hostility as slight and as ineffective as possible.

In the modern world the most important part of this problem arises in youth. If a man is once launched upon the right career and in the right surroundings, he can in most cases escape social persecution, but while he is young and his merits are still untested, he is liable to be at the mercy of ignorant people who consider themselves capable of judging in matters about which they know nothing, and who are outraged at the suggestion that so young a person may know better than they do with all their experience of the world. Many people who have ultimately escaped from the tyranny of ignorance have had so hard a fight and so long a time of repression that in the end they are embittered and their energy is impaired. There is a comfortable doctrine that genius will always make its way, and on the strength of this doctrine many people consider that the persecution of youthful talent cannot do much harm. But there is no ground whatever for accepting this doctrine. It is like the theory that murder will out. Obviously all the murders we know of have been discovered, but who knows how many there may be which have never been heard of? In like manner all the men of genius that we have ever heard of have triumphed over adverse circumstances, but that is no reason for supposing that there were not innumerable others who succumbed in youth. Moreover, it is not a question only of genius, but also of talent, which is just as necessary to the community. And it is not only a question of emerging somehow, but also of emerging unembittered and with unimpaired energy. For all these reasons the way of youth should not be made too hard.

While it is desirable that the old should treat with respect the wishes of the young, it is not desirable that the young should treat with respect the wishes of the old. The reason is simple, namely that in either case it is the lives of the young that are concerned, not the lives of the old. When the young attempt to regulate the lives of the old, as, for example, by objecting to the remarriage of a widowed parent, they are quite as much in the wrong as are the old who attempt to regulate the lives of the young. Old and young alike, as soon as years of discretion have been reached, have a right to their own choices, and if necessary to their own mistakes. Young people are ill-advised if they yield to the pressure of the old in any vital matter. Suppose, for example, that you are a young person who wishes to go on the stage, and that your parents oppose your wish, either on the ground that the stage is immoral or on the ground that it is socially inferior. They may bring every kind of pressure to bear; they may tell you that they will cast you off if you ignore their commands; they may say that you will certainly repent within a few years; they may mention whole strings of horrid examples of young persons who have been rash enough to do what you contemplate doing and came to a bad end in consequence.

They may of course be right in thinking that the stage is not the career for you; it may be that you have no talent for acting, or that you have a bad voice. If this is the case, however, you will soon discover it from theatrical people, and there will still be plenty of time to adopt a different career. The arguments of parents should not be a sufficient reason for relinquishing the attempt. If, in spite of all they say, you carry out your intention, they will soon come round, much sooner in fact than either you or they suppose. If on the other hand you find professional opinion discouraging, that is another matter, for professional opinion must always be treated with respect by beginners.

I think that in general, apart from expert opinion, there is too much respect paid to the opinions of others, both in great matters and in small ones. One should as a rule respect public opinion in so far as is necessary to avoid starvation and to keep out of prison, but anything that goes beyond this is voluntary submission to an unnecessary tyranny, and is likely to interfere with happiness in all kinds of ways. Take, for example, the matter of expenditure. Very many people spend money in ways quite different from those that their natural tastes would enjoin, merely because they feel that the respect of their neighbours depends upon their possession of a good car and their ability to give good dinners. As a matter of fact, any man who can obviously afford a car but genuinely prefers travel or a good library will in the end be much more respected than if he behaved exactly like everyone else. There is, of course, no point in deliberately flouting public opinion; this is still to be under its domination, though in a topsy-turvy way. But to be genuinely indifferent to it is both a strength and a source of happiness. And a society composed of men and women who do not bow too much to the conventions is a far more interesting society than one in which all behave alike. Where each person's character is developed individually, differences of type are preserved, and it is worth while to meet new people, because they are not mere replicas of those whom one has met already. This has been one of the advantages of aristocracy, since where status depended upon birth behaviour was allowed to be erratic. In the modern world we are losing this source of social freedom, and therefore a more deliberate realization of the dangers of uniformity has become desirable. I do not mean that people should be intentionally eccentric, which is just as uninteresting as being conventional. I mean only that people should be natural, and should follow their spontaneous tastes in so far as these are not definitely anti-social.

In the modern world, owing to the swiftness of locomotion, people are less dependent than they used to be upon their geographically nearest neighbours. Those who have cars can regard as a neighbour any person living within twenty miles. They have therefore a much greater power than was formerly the case of choosing their companions. In any populous neighbourhood a man must be very unfortunate if he cannot find congenial souls within twenty miles. The idea that one should know one's immediate neighbours has died out in large centres of population, but still lingers in small towns and in the country. It has become a foolish idea, since there is no need to be dependent upon immediate neighbours for society. More and more it becomes possible to choose our companions on account of congeniality rather than on account of mere propinquity. Happiness is promoted by associations of persons with similar tastes and similar opinions. Social intercourse may be expected to develop more and more along these lines and it may be hoped that by these means the loneliness that now afflicts so many unconventional people will be gradually diminished almost to vanishing point. This will undoubtedly increase their happiness, but it will of course diminish the sadistic pleasure which the conventional at present derive from having the unconventional at their mercy. I do not think, however, that this is a pleasure which we need be greatly concerned to preserve.

Fear of public opinion, like every other form of fear, is oppressive and stunts growth. It is difficult to achieve any kind of greatness while a fear of this kind remains strong, and it is impossible to acquire that freedom of spirit in which true happiness consists, for it is essential to happiness that our way of living should spring from our own deep impulses and not from the accidental tastes and desires of those who happen to be our neighbours, or even our relations. Fear of immediate neighbours is no doubt less than it was, but there is a new kind of fear, namely the fear of what newspapers may say. This is quite as terrifying as anything connected with mediaeval witch-hunts. When the newspaper chooses to make a scapegoat of some perhaps quite harmless person, the results may be very terrible. Fortunately, as yet this is a fate which most people escape through their obscurity, but as publicity gets more and more perfect in its methods, there will be an increasing danger in this novel form of social persecution. This is too grave a matter to be treated with disdain by the individual who is its victim, and whatever may be thought of the great principle of the freedom of the Press, I think the line will have to be drawn more sharply than it is by the existing libel laws, and anything will have to be forbidden that makes life intolerable for innocent individuals, even if they should happen to have done or said things which, published maliciously, can cause them to become unpopular. The only ultimate cure for this evil is, however, an increase of toleration on the part of the public. The best way to increase toleration is to multiply the number of individuals who enjoy real happiness and do not therefore find their chief pleasure in the infliction of pain upon their fellow-men.

PART II
CAUSES OF HAPPINESS

CHAPTER X

Is Happiness Still Possible?

So far we have been considering the unhappy man; we now have the pleasanter task of considering the happy man. From the conversation and the books of some of my friends I have been almost led to conclude that happiness in the modern world has become an impossibility. I find, however, that this view tends to be dissipated by introspection, foreign travel, and the conversation of my gardener. The unhappiness of my literary friends I have considered in an earlier chapter; in the present chapter I wish to make a survey of the happy people that I have come across in the course of my life.

Happiness is of two sorts, though, of course, there are intermediate degrees. The two sorts I mean might be distinguished as plain and fancy, or animal and spiritual, or of the heart and of the head. The designation to be chosen among these alternatives depends, of course, upon the thesis to be proved. I am at the moment not concerned to prove any thesis, but merely to describe. Perhaps the simplest way to describe the difference between the two sorts of happiness is to say that one sort is open to any human being, and the other only to those who can read and write. When I was a boy I knew a man bursting with happiness whose business was digging wells. He was of enormous height and of incredible muscles; he could neither read nor write, and when in the year 1885 he got a vote for Parliament, he learnt for the first time that such an institution existed. His happiness did not depend upon intellectual sources; it was not based upon belief in natural law, or the perfectibility of the species, or the public ownership of public utilities, or the ultimate triumph of the Seventh Day Adventists, or any of the other creeds which intellectuals consider necessary to their enjoyment of life. It was based upon physical vigour, a sufficiency of work, and the overcoming of not insuperable obstacles in the shape of rock. The happiness of my gardener is of the same species; he wages a perennial war against rabbits, of which he speaks exactly as Scotland Yard speaks of Bolsheviks; he considers them dark, designing and ferocious, and is of the opinion that they can only be met by means of a cunning equal to their own. Like the heroes of Valhalla who spent every day hunting a certain wild boar, which they killed every evening but which miraculously came to life again in the morning, my gardener can slay his enemy one day without any fear that the enemy will have disappeared the next day. Although well over seventy, he works all day and bicycles sixteen hilly miles to and from his work, but the fount of joy is inexhaustible, and it is 'they rabbits' that supply it.

But, you will say, these simple delights are not open to superior people like ourselves. What joy can we experience in waging war on such puny creatures as rabbits ? The argument, to my mind, is a poor one. A rabbit is very much larger than a yellow-fever bacillus, and yet a superior person can find happiness in making war upon the latter. Pleasures exactly similar to those of my gardener so far as their emotional content is concerned are open to the most highly educated people. The difference made by education is only in regard to the activities by which these pleasures are to be obtained. Pleasures of achievement demand difficulties such that beforehand success seems doubtful although in the end it is usually achieved. This is perhaps the chief reason why a not excessive estimate of one's own powers is a source of happiness. The man who underestimates himself is perpetually being surprised by success, whereas the man who overestimates himself is just as often surprised by failure. The former kind of surprise is pleasant, the latter unpleasant. It is therefore wise to be not unduly conceited, though also not too modest to be enterprising.

Of the more highly educated sections of the community, the happiest in the present day are the men of science. Many of the most eminent of them are emotionally simple, and obtain from their work a satisfaction so profound that they can derive pleasure from eating and even marrying. Artists and literary men consider it de rigueur to be unhappy in their marriages, but men of science quite frequently remain capable of old-fashioned domestic bliss. The reason of this is that the higher parts of their intelligence are wholly absorbed by their work, and are not allowed to intrude into regions where they have no functions to perform. In their work they are happy because in the modern world science is progressive and powerful, and because its importance is not doubted either by themselves or by laymen. They have therefore no necessity for complex emotions, since the simpler emotions meet with no obstacles. Complexity in emotions is like foam in a river. It is produced by obstacles which break the smoothly flowing current. But so long as the vital energies are unimpeded, they produce no ripple on the surface, and their strength is not evident to the unobservant.

All the conditions of happiness are realized in the life of the man of science. He has an activity which utilizes his abilities to the full, and he achieves results which appear important not only to himself but to the general public, even when it cannot in the smallest degree understand them. In this he is more fortunate than the artist. When the public cannot understand a picture or a poem, they conclude that it is a bad picture or a bad poem. When they cannot understand the theory of relativity they conclude (rightly) that their education has been insufficient. Consequently Einstein is honoured while the best painters are left to starve in garrets, and Einstein is happy while the painters are unhappy. Very few men can be genuinely happy in a life involving continual self-assertion against the scepticism of the mass of mankind, unless they can shut themselves up in a coterie and forget the cold outer world. The man of science has no need of a coterie, since he is thought well of by everybody except his colleagues. The artist, on the contrary, is in the painful situation of having to choose between being despised and being despicable. If his powers are of the first order, he must incur one or the other of these misfortunes—the former if he uses his powers, the latter if he does not. This has not been the case always and everywhere. There have been times when even good artists, even when they were young, were thought well of. Julius II, though he might illtreat Michael Angelo, never supposed him incapable of painting pictures. The modern millionaire, though he may shower wealth upon elderly artists after they have lost their powers, never imagines that their work is as important as his own. Perhaps these circumstances have something to do with the fact that artists are on the average less happy than men of science.

It must, I think, be admitted that the most intelligent young people in Western countries tend to have that kind of unhappiness that comes of finding no adequate employment for their best talents. This, however, is not the case in Eastern countries. The intelligent young at the present day are probably happier in Russia than anywhere else in the world. They have there a new world to create, and an ardent faith in accordance with which to create it. The old have been executed, starved, exiled, or in some other way disinfected, so that they cannot, as in every Western country, compel the young to choose between doing harm and doing nothing. To the sophisticated Occidental the faith of the young Russian may seem crude, but, after all, what is there to be said against it? He *is* creating a new world; the new world is to his liking; the new world will almost certainly, when created, make the average Russian happier than he was before the Revolution. It may not be a world in which the sophisticated Western intellectual would be happy, but the sophisticated Western intellectual does not have to live in it. By any pragmatic test, therefore, the faith of young Russia is justified, and to condemn it as crude can have no justification except on a basis of theory.

In India, China, and Japan, external circumstances of a political sort interfere with the happiness of the young intelligentsia, but there is no such internal obstacle as exists in the West. There are activities which appear important to the young, and, in so far as these activities succeed, the young are happy. They feel that they have an important part to play in the national life, and aims to pursue which, though difficult, are not impossible to realize. Cynicism such as one finds very frequently among the most highly educated young men and women of the West results from the combination of comfort with powerlessness. Powerlessness makes people feel that nothing is worth doing, and comfort makes the painfulness of this feeling just endurable. Throughout the East the University student can hope for more influence upon public opinion than he can have in the modern West, but he has much less opportunity than in the West of securing a substantial income. Being neither powerless nor comfortable, he becomes a reformer or a revolutionary, not a cynic. The happiness of the reformer or revolutionary depends upon the course of public affairs, but probably even while he is being executed he enjoys more real happiness than is possible for the comfortable cynic. I remember a young Chinese visitor to my school who was going home to found a similar school in a reactionary part of China. He expected the result to be that his head would be cut off. Nevertheless he enjoyed a quiet happiness that I could only envy.

I do not wish to suggest, however, that these high-flown kinds of happiness are the only possible ones. They are in fact open only to a minority, since they require a kind of ability and a width of interest which cannot be very common. It is not only eminent scientists who can derive pleasure through work, nor is it only leading statesmen who can derive pleasure through advocacy of a cause. The pleasure of work is open to anyone who can develop some specialized skill, provided that he can get satisfaction from the exercise of his skill without demanding universal applause. I knew a man who had lost the use of both legs in early youth, but he had remained serenely happy throughout a long life; he had achieved this by writing a work in five volumes on rose blight, on which I always understood he was the leading expert. I have not had the pleasure of knowing any large number of conchologists, but from those who have I have always understood that the study of shells brings contentment to those who engage in it. I knew a man once who was the best compositor in the world, and was sought out by all those who devoted themselves to inventing artistic types; he derived joy, not so much from the very genuine respect in which he was held by persons whose respect was not lightly bestowed, as from the actual delight in the exercise of his craft, a delight not wholly unlike that which good dancers derive from dancing. I have known also compositors who were experts in setting up mathematical type, or Nestorian script, or cuneiform, or anything else that was out of the way and difficult. I did not discover whether these men's private lives were happy, but in their working hours their constructive instincts were fully gratified.

It is customary to say that in our machine age there is less room than formerly for the craftsman's joy in skilled work. I am not at all

D

sure that this is true: the skilled workman nowadays works, it is true, at quite different things from those that occupied the attention of the mediaeval guilds, but he is still very important and quite essential in the machine economy. There are those who make scientific instruments and delicate machines, there are designers, there are aeroplane mechanics, chauffeurs, and hosts of others who have a trade in which skill can be developed to almost any extent. The agricultural labourer and the peasant in comparatively primitive communities is not, so far as I have been able to observe, nearly as happy as a chauffeur or an engine-driver. It is true that the work of the peasant who cultivates his own land is varied; he ploughs, he sows, he reaps. But he is at the mercy of the elements, and is very conscious of his dependence, whereas the man who works a modern mechanism is conscious of power, and acquires the sense that man is the master, not the slave, of natural forces. It is true, of course, that work is very uninteresting to the large body of mere machine-minders who repeat some mechanical operation over and over again with the minimum of variation, but the more uninteresting the work becomes, the more possible it is to get it performed by a machine. The ultimate goal of machine production—from which, it is true, we are as yet far removed—is a system in which everything uninteresting is done by machines, and human beings are reserved for the work involving variety and initiative. In such a world the work will be less boring and less depressing than it has been at any time since the introduction of agriculture. In taking to agriculture mankind decided that they would submit to monotony and tedium in order to diminish the risk of starvation. When men obtained their food by hunting, work was a joy, as one can see from the fact that the rich still pursue these ancestral occupations for amusement. But with the introduction of agriculture mankind entered upon a long period of meanness, misery, and madness, from which they are only now being freed by the beneficent operation of the machine. It is all very well for sentimentalists to speak of contact with the soil and the ripe wisdom of Hardy's philosophic peasants, but the one desire of every young man in the countryside is to find work in towns where he can escape from the slavery of wind and weather and the solitude of dark winter evenings into the reliable and human atmosphere of the factory and the cinema. Companionship and co-operation are essential elements in the happiness of the average man, and these are to be obtained in industry far more fully than in agriculture.

Belief in a cause is a source of happiness to large numbers of people. I am not thinking only of revolutionaries, socialists, nationalists in oppressed countries, and such; I am thinking also of many humbler kinds of belief. The men I have known who believed that the English were the lost ten tribes were almost invariably happy, while as for those who believed that the English were only the tribes of Ephraim and Manasseh, their bliss knew no bounds. I am not suggesting that the reader should adopt this creed, since I cannot advocate any happiness based upon what seem to me to be false beliefs. For the same reason I cannot urge the reader to believe that men should live exclusively upon nuts, although, so far as my observation goes, this belief invariably ensures perfect happiness. But it is easy to find some cause which is in no degree fantastic, and those whose interest in any such cause is genuine are provided with an occupation for their leisure hours and a complete antidote to the feeling that life is empty.

Not so very far removed from the devotion to obscure causes is absorption in a hobby. One of the most eminent of living mathematicians divides his time equally between mathematics and stamp-collecting. I imagine that the latter affords consolation at the moments when he can make no progress with the former. The difficulty of proving propositions in the theory of numbers is not the only sorrow that stamp-collecting can cure, nor are stamps the only things that can be collected. Consider what a vast field of ecstasy opens before the imagination when one thinks of old china, snuff-boxes, Roman coins, arrow-heads, and flint implements. It is true that many of us are too 'superior' for these simple pleasures. We have all experienced them in boyhood, but have thought them, for some reason, unworthy of a grown man. This is a complete mistake; any pleasure that does no harm to other people is to be valued. For my part, I collect rivers: I derive pleasure from having gone down the Volga and up the Yangtse, and regret very much having never seen the Amazon or the Orinoco. Simple as these emotions are, I am not ashamed of them. Or consider again the passionate joy of the baseball fan: he turns to his newspaper with avidity, and the radio affords him the keenest thrills. I remember meeting for the first time one of the leading literary men of America, a man whom I had supposed from his books to be filled with melancholy. But it so happened that at that moment the most crucial baseball results were coming through on the radio; he forgot me, literature, and all the other sorrows of our sublunary life, and yelled with joy as his favourites achieved victory. Ever since this incident I have been able to read his books without feeling depressed by the misfortunes of his characters.

Fads and hobbies, however, are in many cases, perhaps most, not a source of fundamental happiness, but a means of escape from reality, of forgetting for the moment some pain too difficult to be faced. Fundamental happiness depends more than anything else upon what may be called a friendly interest in persons and things.

A friendly interest in persons is a form of affectionateness, but not the form which is grasping and possessive and seeking always an emphatic response. This latter form is very frequently a source of unhappiness. The kind that makes for happiness is the kind that likes to observe people and finds pleasure in their individual traits, that wishes to afford scope for the interests and pleasures of those with whom it is brought into contact without desiring to acquire power over them or to secure their enthusiastic admiration. The person whose attitude towards others is genuinely of this kind will be a source of happiness and a recipient of reciprocal kindness. His relations with others, whether slight or serious, will satisfy both his interests and his affections; he will not be soured by ingratitude, since he will seldom suffer it and will not notice when he does. The same idiosyncrasies which would get on another man's nerves to the point of exasperation will be to him a source of gentle amusement. He will achieve without effort results which another man, after long struggles, will find to be unattainable. Being happy in himself, he will be a pleasant companion, and this in turn will increase his happiness. But all this must be genuine; it must not spring from an idea of self-sacrifice inspired by a sense of duty. A sense of duty is useful in work, but offensive in personal relations. People wish to be liked, not to be endured with patient resignation. To like many people spontaneously and without effort is perhaps the greatest of all sources of personal happiness.

I spoke also in the last paragraph of what I call a friendly interest in things. This phrase may perhaps seem forced; it may be said that it is impossible to feel friendly to things. Nevertheless, there is something analogous to friendliness in the kind of interest that a geologist takes in rocks, or an archaeologist in ruins, and this interest ought to be an element in our attitude to individuals or societies. It is possible to have an interest in things which is hostile rather than friendly. A man might collect facts concerning the habitats of spiders because he hated spiders and wished to live where they were few. This kind of interest would not afford the same satisfaction as the geologist derives from his rocks. An interest in impersonal things, though perhaps less valuable as an ingredient in everyday happiness than a friendly attitude towards our fellow creatures, is nevertheless very important. The world is vast and our own powers are limited. If all our happiness is bound up entirely in our personal circumstances it is difficult not to demand of life more than it has to give. And to demand too much is the surest way of getting even less than is possible. The man who can forget his worries by means of a genuine interest in, say, the Council of Trent, or the life history of stars, will find that, when he returns from his excursion into the impersonal world, he has acquired a poise and calm which enable him to deal with his worries in the best way, and he will in the meantime have experienced a genuine even if temporary happiness.

The secret of happiness is this: let your interests be as wide as possible, and let your reactions to the things and persons that interest you be as far as possible friendly rather than hostile.

This preliminary survey of the possibilities of happiness will be expanded in subsequent chapters, together with suggestions as to ways of escaping from psychological sources of misery.

CHAPTER XI

Zest

IN this chapter I propose to deal with what seems to me the most universal and distinctive mark of happy men, namely zest.

Perhaps the best way to understand what is meant by zest will be to consider the different ways in which men behave when they sit down to a meal. There are those to whom a meal is merely a bore; no matter how excellent the food may be, they feel that it is uninteresting. They have had excellent food before, probably at almost every meal they have eaten. They have never known what it was to go without a meal until hunger became a raging passion, but have come to regard meals as merely conventional occurrences, dictated by the fashions of the society in which they live. Like everything else, meals are tiresome, but it is no use to make a fuss, because nothing else will be less tiresome. Then there are the invalids who eat from a sense of duty, because the doctor has told them that it is necessary to take a little nourishment in order to keep up their strength. Then there are the epicures, who start hopefully, but find that nothing has been quite so well cooked as it ought to have been. Then there are the gormandizers, who fall upon their food with eager rapacity, eat too much, and grow plethoric and stertorous. Finally there are those who begin with a sound appetite, are glad of their food, eat until they have had enough, and then stop. Those who are set down before the feast of life have similar attitudes towards the good things which it offers. The happy man corresponds to the last of our eaters. What hunger is in relation to food, zest is in relation to life. The man who is bored with his meals corresponds to the victim of Byronic unhappiness. The invalid who eats from a sense of duty corresponds to the ascetic, the gormandizer to the voluptuary. The epicure corresponds to the fastidious person who condemns half the pleasures of life as unaesthetic. Oddly enough, all these types, with the possible exception of the gormandizer, feel contempt for the man of healthy appetite and consider themselves his superior. It seems to them vulgar to enjoy food because you are hungry or to enjoy life because it offers a variety of interesting spectacles and surprising experiences. From the height of their disillusionment they look down upon those whom they despise as simple souls. For my part I have no sympathy with this outlook. All disenchantment is to me a malady, which, it is true, certain circumstances may render inevitable, but which none the less, when it occurs, is to be cured as soon as possible, not to be regarded as a higher form of wisdom. Suppose one man likes strawberries and another does not; in what respect is the latter superior? There is no abstract and impersonal proof either that strawberries are good or that they are not good. To the man who likes them they are good; to the man who dislikes them they are not. But the man who likes them has a pleasure which the other does not have; to that extent his life is more enjoyable and he is better adapted to the world in which both must live. What is true in this trivial instance is equally true in more important matters. The man who enjoys watching football is to that extent superior to the man who does not. The man who enjoys reading is still more superior to the man who does not, since opportunities for reading are more frequent than opportunities for watching football. The more things a man is interested in, the more opportunities of happiness he has, and the less he is at the mercy of fate, since if he loses one thing he can fall back upon another. Life is too short to be interested in everything, but it is good to be interested in as many things as are necessary to fill our days. We are all prone to the malady of the introvert, who, with the manifold spectacle of the world spread out before him, turns away and gazes only upon the emptiness within. But let us not imagine that there is anything grand about the introvert's unhappiness.

There were once upon a time two sausage machines, exquisitely constructed for the purpose of turning pig into the most delicious sausages. One of these retained his zest for pig and produced sausages innumerable; the other said: 'What is pig to me? My own works are far more interesting and wonderful than any pig.' He refused pig and set to work to study his inside. When bereft of its natural food, his inside ceased to function, and the more he studied it, the more empty and foolish it seemed to him to be. All the exquisite apparatus by which the delicious transformation had hitherto been made stood still, and he was at a loss to guess what it was capable of doing. This second sausage machine was like the man who has lost his zest, while the first was like the man who has retained it. The mind is a strange machine which can combine the materials offered to it in the most astonishing ways, but without materials from the external world it is powerless, and unlike the sausage machine it must seize its materials for itself, since events only become experiences through the interest that we take in them: if they do not interest us, we are making nothing of them. The man, therefore, whose attention is turned within finds nothing worthy of his notice, whereas the man whose attention is turned outward can find within, in those rare moments when he examines his soul, the most varied and interesting assortment of ingredients being dissected and recombined into beautiful or instructive patterns.

The forms of zest are innumerable. Sherlock Holmes, it may be remembered, picked up a hat which he happened to find lying in the street. After looking at it for a moment he remarked that its owner had come down in the world as the result of drink, and that his wife was no longer so fond of him as she used to be. Life could never be boring to a man to whom casual objects offered such a wealth of interest. Think of the different things that may be noticed in the course of a country walk. One man may be interested in the birds, another in the vegetation, another in the geology, yet another in the agriculture, and so on. Any one of these things is interesting if it interests you, and, other things being equal, the man who is interested in any one of them is a man better adapted to the world than the man who is not interested.

How extraordinarily different, again, are the attitudes of different people to their fellow-men. One man, in the course of a long train journey, will fail entirely to observe any of his fellow travellers while another will have summed them all up, analysed their characters, made a shrewd guess at their circumstances, and perhaps even ascertained the most secret histories of several of them. People differ just as much in what they feel towards others as in what they ascertain about them. Some men find almost everybody boring, others quickly and easily develop a friendly feeling towards those with whom they are brought in contact, unless there is some definite reason for feeling otherwise. Take again such a matter as travel: some men will travel through many countries, going always to the best hotels, eating exactly the same food as they would eat at home, meeting the same idle rich whom they would meet at home, conversing on the same topics upon which they converse at their own dinner-table. When they return, their only feeling is one of relief at having done with the boredom of expensive locomotion. Other men wherever they go see what is characteristic, make the acquaintance of people who typify the locality, observe whatever is of interest either historically or socially, eat the food of the country, learn its manners and its language, and come home with a new stock of pleasant thoughts for winter evenings.

In all these different situations the man who has the zest for life has the advantage over the man who has none. Even unpleasant experiences have their uses to him. I am glad to have smelt a Chinese crowd and a Sicilian village, though I cannot pretend that my pleasure was very great at the moment. Adventurous men enjoy shipwrecks, mutinies, earthquakes, conflagrations, and all kinds of unpleasant experiences, provided they do not go so far as to impair health. They say to themselves in an earthquake, for example, 'So that is what an earthquake is like', and it gives them pleasure to have their knowledge of the world increased by this new item. It would not be true to say that such men are not at the mercy of fate, for if they should lose their health they would be very likely to lose their zest at the same time, though this is by no means certain. I have known men die at the end of years of slow torture, and yet retain their zest almost till the last moment. Some forms of ill-health destroy zest, others do not. I do not know whether the biochemists are able as yet to distinguish between these kinds. Perhaps when biochemistry has made further advances we shall be able to take tablets that will ensure our feeling an interest in everything, but until that day comes we are compelled to depend upon common-sense observation of life to judge what are the causes that enable some men to take an interest in every-thing, while compelling others to take an interest in nothing.

Zest is sometimes general, sometimes specialized. It may be very specialized indeed. Readers of Borrow may remember a character who occurs in *Romany Rye*. He had lost his wife, to whom he was devoted, and felt for a time that life had grown utterly barren. But he became interested in Chinese inscriptions on teapots and tea-chests, and by the aid of a French Chinese grammar, after learning French for the purpose, gradually managed to decipher them, thereby acquiring a new interest in life though he never used his Chinese knowledge for other purposes. I have known men who were entirely absorbed in the endeavour to find out all about the Gnostic heresy, and other men whose principal interest lay in collating the manuscripts and early editions of Hobbes. It is quite impossible to guess in advance what will interest a man, but most men are capable of a keen interest in something or other, and when once such an interest has been aroused their life becomes free from tedium. Very specialized interests are, however, a less satisfactory source of happiness than a general zest for life, since they can hardly fill the whole of a man's time, and there is always the danger that he may come to know all there is to know about the particular matter that has become his hobby.

It will be remembered that among our different types at the banquet we included the gormandizer, whom we were not prepared to praise. The reader may think that the man with zest whom we have been praising does not differ in any definable way from the gormandizer. The time has come when we must try to make the distinction between the two types more definite.

The ancients, as everyone knows, regarded moderation as one of the essential virtues. Under the influence of romanticism and the French Revolution this view was abandoned by many, and overmastering passions were admired, even if, like those of Byron's heroes, they were of a destructive and anti-social kind. The ancients, however, were clearly in the right. In the good life there must be a balance between different activities, and no one of them must be carried so far as to make the others impossible. The gormandizer sacrifices all other pleasures to that of eating, and by so doing diminishes the total happiness of his life. Many other passions besides eating may be carried to a like excess. The

Empress Josephine was a gormandizer in regard to clothes. At first Napoleon used to pay her dressmaker's bills, though with continually increasing protest. At last he told her that she really must learn moderation, and that in future he would only pay her bills when the amount seemed reasonable. When her next dressmaker's bill came in, she was for a moment at her wits' end, but presently she bethought herself of a scheme. She went to the War Minister and demanded that he should pay her bill out of the funds provided for the war. Since he knew that she had the power to get him dismissed, he did so, and the French lost Genoa in consequence. So at least some books say, though I am not prepared to vouch for the exact truth of the story. For our purpose it is equally apt whether true or an exaggeration, since it serves to show how far the passion for clothes may carry a woman who has the opportunity to indulge it. Dipsomaniacs and nymphomaniacs are obvious examples of the same kind of thing. The principle in these matters is fairly obvious. All our separate tastes and desires have to fit into the general framework of life. If they are to be a source of happiness they must be compatible with health, with the affection of those whom we love, and with the respect of the society in which we live. Some passions can be indulged to almost any extent without passing beyond these limits, others cannot. The man, let us say, who loves chess, if he happens to be a bachelor with independent means, need not restrict his passion in any degree, whereas if he has a wife and children and no independent means, he will have to restrict it very severely. The dipsomaniac and the gormandizer, even if they have no social ties, are unwise from a self-regarding point of view, since their indulgence interferes with health, and gives them hours of misery in return for minutes of pleasure. Certain things form a framework within which any separate passion must live if it is not to become a source of misery. Such things are health, the general possession of one's faculties, a sufficient income to provide for necessaries, and the most essential social duties, such as those towards wife and children. The man who sacrifices these things for chess is essentially as bad as the dipsomaniac. The only reason we do not condemn him so severely is that he is much less common, and that only a man of somewhat rare abilities is likely to be carried away by absorption in so intellectual a game. The Greek formula of moderation practically covers these cases. The man who likes chess sufficiently to look forward throughout his working day to the game that he will play in the evening is fortunate, but the man who gives up work in order to play chess all day has lost the virtue of moderation. It is recorded that Tolstoy, in his younger and unregenerate days, was awarded the military cross for valour in the field, but when the time came for him to be presented with it, he was so absorbed in a game of chess that he decided not to go. We can hardly find fault with Tolstoy on this account, since to him it might well be a matter of indifference whether he won military decorations or not, but in a lesser man such an act would have been one of folly.

As a limitation upon the doctrine that has just been set forth, it ought to be admitted that some performances are considered so essentially noble as to justify the sacrifice of everything else on their behalf. The man who loses his life in the defence of his country is not blamed if thereby his wife and children are left penniless. The man who is engaged in experiments with a view to some great scientific discovery or invention is not blamed afterwards for the poverty that he has made his family endure, provided that his efforts are crowned with ultimate success. If, however, he never succeeds in making the discovery or the invention that he was attempting, public opinion condemns him as a crank, which seems unfair, since no one in such an enterprise can be sure of success in advance. During the first millennium of the Christian era a man who abandoned his family for a saintly life was praised, though nowadays it would be held that he ought to make some provision for them.

I think there is always some deep-seated psychological difference between the gormandizer and the man of healthy appetite. The man in whom one desire runs to excess at the expense of all others is usually a man with some deep-seated trouble, who is seeking to escape from a spectre. In the case of the dipsomaniac this is obvious: men drink in order to forget. If they had no spectres in their lives, they would not find drunkenness more agreeable than sobriety. As the legendary Chinaman said: 'Me no drinkee for drinkee, me drinkee for drunkee.' This is typical of all excessive and one-sided passions. It is not pleasure in the object itself that is sought, but oblivion. There is, however, a very great difference according as oblivion is sought in a sottish manner or by the exercise of faculties in themselves desirable. Borrow's friend who taught himself Chinese in order to be able to endure the loss of his wife was seeking oblivion, but he sought it in an activity that had no harmful effects, but on the contrary improved his intelligence and his knowledge. Against such forms of escape there is nothing to be said. It is otherwise with the man who seeks oblivion in drinking or gambling or any other form of unprofitable excitement. There are, it is true, border-line cases. What should we say of the man who runs mad risks in aeroplanes or on mountain tops, because life has become irksome to him? If his risks serve any public object, we may admire him, but if not, we shall have to place him only slightly above the gambler and drunkard.

Genuine zest, not the sort that is really a search for oblivion, is part of the natural make-up of human beings except in so far as it has been destroyed by unfortunate circumstances. Young children are interested in everything that they see and hear; the world is full of surprises to them, and they are perpetually engaged with ardour in the pursuit of knowledge, not, of course, of scholastic knowledge, but of the sort that consists in acquiring familiarity with the objects that attract their attention. Animals, even when adult, retain their zest provided they are in health. A cat in an unfamiliar room will not sit down until it has sniffed at every corner on the off-chance that there may be a smell of mouse somewhere. The man who has never been fundamentally thwarted will retain his natural interest in the external world, and so long as he retains it he will find life pleasant unless his liberty is unduly curtailed. Loss of zest in civilized society is very largely due to the restrictions upon liberty which are essential to our way of life. The savage hunts when he is hungry, and in so doing is obeying a direct impulse. The man who goes to his work every morning at a certain hour is actuated fundamentally by the same impulse, namely the need to secure a living, but in his case the impulse does not operate directly and at the moment when it is felt: it operates indirectly through abstractions, beliefs and volitions. At the moment when the man starts off to his work he is not feeling hungry, since he has just had his breakfast. He merely knows that hunger will recur, and that going to his work is a means of satisfying future hunger. Impulses are irregular, whereas habits, in a civilized society, have to be regular. Among savages, even collective enterprizes, in so far as they exist, are spontaneous and impulsive. When the tribe is going to war the tom-tom rouses military ardour, and herd excitement inspires each individual to the necessary activity. Modern enterprizes cannot be managed in this way. When a train has to be started at a given moment it is impossible to inspire the porters, the engine-driver, and the signalman by means of barbaric music. They must each do their job merely because it has to be done; their motive, that is to say, is indirect: they have no impulse towards the activity, but only towards the ultimate reward of the activity. A great deal of social life has the same defect. People converse with each other, not from any wish to do so, but because of some ultimate benefit that they hope to derive from co-operation. At every moment of life the civilized man is hedged about by restrictions of impulse: if he happens to feel cheerful he must not sing or dance in the street, while if he happens to feel sad he must not sit on the pavement and weep, for fear of obstructing pedestrian traffic. In youth his liberty is restricted at school, in adult life it is restricted throughout his working hours. All this makes zest more difficult to retain, for the continual restraint tends to produce weariness and boredom. Nevertheless, a civilized society is impossible without a very considerable degree of restraint upon spontaneous impulse, since spontaneous impulse will only produce the simplest forms of social co-operation, not those highly complex forms which modern economic organization demands. In order to rise above these obstacles to zest a man needs health and superabundant energy, or else, if he has that good fortune, work that he finds interesting on its own account. Health, so far as statistics can show, has been steadily improving in all civilized countries during the last hundred years, but energy is more difficult to measure, and I am doubtful whether physical vigour in moments of health is as great as it was formerly. The problem here is to a great extent a social problem, and as such I do not propose to discuss it in the present volume. The problem has, however, a personal and psychological aspect which we have already discussed in connection with fatigue. Some men retain their zest in spite of the handicaps of civilized life, and many men could do so if they were free from the inner psychological conflicts upon which a great part of their energy is expended. Zest demands energy more than that sufficient for the necessary work, and this in turn demands the smooth working of the psychological machine. Of the causes promoting the smooth working I shall have more to say in later chapters.

In women, less nowadays than formerly, but still to a very large extent, zest has been greatly diminished by a mistaken conception of respectability. It was thought undersirable that women should take an obvious interest in men, or that they should display too much vivacity in public. In learning not to be interested in men they learned very frequently to be interested in nothing, or at any rate in nothing except a certain kind of correct behaviour. To teach an attitude of inactivity and withdrawal towards life is clearly to teach something very inimical to zest, and to encourage a certain kind of absorption in self which is characteristic of highly respectable women, especially when they are uneducated. They do not have the interest in sport that average men have, they care nothing about politics, towards men their attitude is one of prim aloofness, towards women their attitude is one of veiled hostility based upon the conviction that other women are less respectable than they are themselves. They boast that they keep themselves to themselves; that is to say, their lack of interest in their fellow creatures appears to them in the light of a virtue. For this, of course, they are not to blame; they are only accepting the moral teaching that has been current for thousands of years where women are concerned. They are, however, victims, much to be pitied, of a system of repression whose iniquity they have failed to perceive. To such women all that is ungenerous appears good and all that is generous appears evil. In their own social circle they do what they can to kill joy, in politics they love repressive legislation. Fortunately the type is growing less common, but it is still far more prevalent than is supposed by those who live in emancipated circles. I recommend anyone who doubts this statement to go the round of a number of lodging-houses seeking a lodging, and to take note of the landladies that he will meet during his search. He will find that they are living by a conception of female excellence which involves as an essential part the destruction of all zest for life, and that their minds and hearts are dwarfed and stunted as a result. Between male and female excellence rightly conceived there is no difference, or at any rate no difference such as tradition inculcates. For women as for men zest is the secret of happiness and well-being.

CHAPTER XII

Affection

ONE of the chief causes of lack of zest is the feeling that one is unloved, whereas conversely the feeling of being loved promotes zest more than anything else does. A man may have the feeling of being unloved for a variety of reasons. He may consider himself such a dreadful person that no one could possibly love him; he may in childhood have had to accustom himself to receiving less love than fell to the share of other children; or he may in fact be a person whom nobody loves. But in this latter event the cause probably lies in a lack of self-confidence due to early misfortune. The man who feels himself unloved may take various attitudes as a result. He may make desperate efforts to win affection, probably by means of exceptional acts of kindness. In this, however, he is very likely to be unsuccessful, since the motive of the kindnesses is easily perceived by their beneficiaries, and human nature is so constructed that it gives affection most readily to those who seem least to demand it. The man, therefore, who endeavours to purchase affection by benevolent actions becomes disillusioned by experience of human ingratitude. It never occurs to him that the affection which he is trying to buy is of far more value than the material benefits which he offers as its price, and yet the feeling that this is so is at the basis of his actions. Another man, observing that he is unloved, may seek revenge upon the world, either by stirring up wars and revolutions, or by a pen dipped in gall, like Dean Swift. This is an heroic reaction to misfortune, requiring a force of character sufficient to enable a man to pit himself against the rest of the world. Few men are able to reach such heights; the great majority, both of men and women, if they feel themselves unloved, sink into a timid despair relieved only by occasional gleams of envy and malice. As a rule, the lives of such people become extremely self-centred, and the absence of affection gives them a sense of insecurity from which they instinctively seek to escape by allowing habit to dominate their lives utterly and completely. For those who make themselves the slaves of unvarying routine are generally actuated by fear of a cold outer world, and by the feeling that they will not bump into it if they walk along the same paths that they have walked along on previous days.

Those who face life with a feeling of security are much happier than those who face it with a feeling of insecurity, at any rate so long as their sense of security does not lead them to disaster. And in a very great many cases, though not in all, a sense of security will itself help a man to escape dangers to which another would succumb. If you are walking over a chasm on a narrow plank, you are much more likely to fall if you feel fear than if you do not. And the same thing applies to the conduct of life. The fearless man may, of course, meet with sudden disaster, but it is likely that he will pass unscathed through many difficult situations in which a timid man would come to grief. This useful kind of self-confidence has, of course, innumerable forms. One man is confident on mountains, another on the sea, and yet another in the air. But general self-confidence towards life comes more than anything else from being accustomed to receive as much of the right sort of affection as one has need for. And it is this habit of mind considered as a source of zest that I wish to speak about in the present chapter.

It is affection received, not affection given, that causes this sense of security, though it arises most of all from affection which is reciprocal. Strictly speaking, it is not only affection but also admiration that has this effect. Persons whose trade is to secure public admiration, such as actors, preachers, speakers, and politicians, come to depend more and more upon applause. When they receive their due meed of public approbation their life is full of zest; when they do not, they become discontented and self-centred. The diffused good will of a multitude does for them what is done for others by the more concentrated affection of the few. The child whose parents are fond of him accepts their affection as a law of nature. He does not think very much about it, although it is of great importance to his happiness. He thinks about the world, about the adventures that come his way and the more marvellous adventures that will come his way when he is grown up. But behind all these external interests there is the feeling that he will be protected from disaster by parental affection. The child from whom for any reason parental affection is withdrawn is likely to become timid and unadventurous, filled with fears and self-pity, and no longer able to meet the world in a mood of gay exploration. Such a child may set to work at a surprisingly early age to meditate on life and death and human destiny. He becomes an introvert, melancholy at first, but seeking ultimately the unreal consolations of some system of philosophy or theology. The world is a higgledy-piggledy place, containing things pleasant and things unpleasant in haphazard sequence. And the desire to make an intelligible system or pattern out of it is at bottom an outcome of fear, in fact a kind of agoraphobia or dread of open spaces. Within the four walls of his library the timid student feels safe. If he can persuade himself that the universe is equally tidy, he can feel almost equally safe when he has to venture forth into the streets. Such a man, if he had received more affection, would have feared the real world less, and would not have had to invent an ideal world to take its place in his beliefs.

By no means all affection, however, has this effect in encouraging adventurousness. The affection given must be itself robust rather than timid, desiring excellence even more than safety on the part of its object, though of course by no means indifferent to safety. The timid mother or nurse, who is perpetually warning children against disasters that may occur, who thinks that every dog will bite and that every cow is a bull, may produce in them a timidity equal to her own, and may cause them to feel that they are never safe except in her immediate neighbourhood. To the unduly possessive mother this feeling on the part of a child may be agreeable: she may desire his dependence upon herself more than his capacity to cope with the world. In that case her child is probably worse off in the long run than he would be if he were not loved at all. The habits of mind formed in early years are likely to persist through life. Many people when they fall in love look for a little haven of refuge from the world, where they can be sure of being admired when they are not admirable, and praised when they are not praiseworthy. To many men home is a refuge from the truth: it is their fears and their timidities that make them enjoy a companionship in which these feelings are put to rest. They seek from their wives what they obtained formerly from an unwise mother, and yet they are surprised if their wives regard them as grown-up children.

To define the best kind of affection is not altogether easy, since clearly there will be *some* protective element in it. We do not feel indifferent to the hurts of people whom we love. I think, however, that apprehension of misfortune, as opposed to sympathy with a misfortune that has actually occurred, should play as small a part as possible in affection. Fear for others is only a shade better than fear for ourselves. Moreover it is very often a camouflage for possessiveness. It is hoped that by rousing their fears a more complete empire over them can be obtained. This, of course, is one of the reasons why men have liked timid women, since by protecting them they came to own them. The amount of solicitude of which a person can be the object without damage to himself depends upon his character: a person who is hardy and adventurous can endure a great deal without damage, whereas a timid person should be encouraged to expect little in this way.

Affection received has a twofold function. We have spoken of it hitherto in connection with security, but in adult life it has even an more essential biological purpose, namely parenthood. To be unable to inspire sex love is a grave misfortune to any man or woman, since it deprives him or her of the greatest joys that life has to offer. This deprivation is almost sure sooner or later to destroy zest and produce introversion. Very frequently, however, previous misfortunes in childhood have produced defects of character which are the cause of failure to obtain love in later years. This is perhaps more true where men are concerned than it is as regards women, for on the whole women tend to love men for their character while men tend to love women for their appearance. In this respect, it must be said, men show themselves the inferiors of women, for the qualities that men find pleasing in women are on the whole less desirable than those that women find pleasing in men. I am not at all sure, however, that it is easier to acquire a good character than a good appearance; at any rate, the steps necessary for the latter are better understood and more readily pursued by women than are the steps necessary for the former by men.

We have been speaking hitherto of the affection of which a

person is the object. I wish now to speak of the affection that a person gives. This also is of two different kinds, one of which is perhaps the most important expression of a zest for life, while the other is an expression of fear. The former seems to me wholly admirable, while the latter is at best a consolation. If you are sailing in a ship on a fine day along a beautiful coast, you admire the coast and feel pleasure in it. This pleasure is one derived entirely from looking outward, and has nothing to do with any desperate need of your own. If, on the other hand, your ship is wrecked and you swim towards the coast, you acquire for it a new kind of love: it represents security against the waves, and its beauty or ugliness becomes an unimportant matter. The better sort of affection corresponds to the feeling of the man whose ship is secure, the less excellent sort corresponds to that of the shipwrecked swimmer. The first of these kinds of affection is only possible in so far as a man feels safe, or at any rate is indifferent to such dangers as beset him; the latter kind, on the contrary, is caused by the feeling of insecurity. The feeling caused by insecurity is much more subjective and self-centred than the other, since the loved person is valued for services rendered, not for intrinsic qualities. I do not, however, wish to suggest that this kind of affection has no legitimate part to play in life. In fact, almost all real affection contains something of both kinds in combination, and in so far as affection does really cure the sense of insecurity it sets a man free to feel again that interest in the world which in moments of danger and fear is obscured. But while recognizing the part that such affection has to play in life, we must still hold that it is less excellent than the other kind, since it depends upon fear, and fear is an evil, and also because it is more self-centred. In the best kind of affection a man hopes for a new happiness rather than for escape from an old unhappiness.

The best type of affection is reciprocally life-giving; each receives affection with joy and gives it without effort, and each finds the whole world more interesting in consequence of the existence of this reciprocal happiness. There is, however, another kind, by no means uncommon, in which one person sucks the vitality of the other, one receives what the other gives, but gives almost nothing in return. Some very vital people belong to this bloodsucking type. They extract the vitality from one victim after another, but while they prosper and grow interesting, those upon whom they live grow pale and dim and dull. Such people use others as means to their own ends, and never consider them as ends in themselves. Fundamentally they are not interested in those whom for the moment they think they love; they are interested only in the stimulus to their own activities, perhaps of a quite impersonal sort. Evidently this springs from some defect in their nature, but it is one not altogether easy either to diagnose or to cure. It is a characteristic frequently associated with great ambition, and is rooted, I should say, in an unduly one-sided view of what makes human happiness. Affection in the sense of a genuine reciprocal interest of two persons in each other, not solely as means to each other's good, but rather as a combination having a common good, is one of the most important elements of real happiness, and the man whose ego is so enclosed within steel walls that this enlargement of it is impossible misses the best that life has to offer, however successful he may be in his career. Ambition which excludes affection from its purview is generally the result of some kind of anger or hatred against the human race, produced by unhappiness in youth, by injustices in later life, or by any of the causes which lead to persecution mania. A too powerful ego is a prison from which a man must escape if he is to enjoy the world to the full. A capacity for genuine affection is one of the marks of the man who has escaped from this prison of self. To receive affection is by no means enough; affection which is received should liberate the affection which is to be given, and only where both exist in equal measure does affection achieve its best possibilities.

Obstacles, psychological and social, to the blossoming of reciprocal affection are a grave evil, from which the world has always suffered and still suffers. People are slow to give admiration for fear it should be misplaced; they are slow to bestow affection for fear that they should be made to suffer either by the person upon whom they bestow it or by a censorious world. Caution is enjoined both in the name of morality and in the name of worldly wisdom, with the result that generosity and adventurousness are discouraged where the affections are concerned. All this tends to produce timidity and anger against mankind, since many people miss throughout life what is really a fundamental need, and to nine out of ten an indispensable condition of a happy and expansive attitude towards the world. It is not to be supposed that those who are what is called immoral are in this respect superior to those who are not. In sex relations there is very often almost nothing that can be called real affection; not infrequently there is even a fundamental hostility. Each is trying not to give himself or herself away, each is preserving fundamental loneliness, each remains intact and therefore unfructified. In such experiences there is no fundamental value. I do not say that they should be carefully avoided, since the steps necessary to this end would be likely to interfere also with the occasions where a more valuable and profound affection could grow up. But I do say that the only sex relations that have real value are those in which there is no reticence and in which the whole personality of both becomes merged in a new collective personality. Of all forms of caution, caution in love is perhaps the most fatal to true happiness.

CHAPTER XIII

The Family

OF all the institutions that have come down to us from the past none is in the present day so disorganized and derailed as the family. Affection of parents for children and of children for parents is capable of being one of the greatest sources of happiness, but in fact at the present day the relations of parents and children are, in nine cases out of ten, a source of unhappiness to both parties, and in ninety-nine cases out of a hundred a source of unhappiness to at least one of the two parties. This failure of the family to provide the fundamental satisfaction which in principle it is capable of yielding is one of the most deep-seated causes of the discontent which is prevalent in our age. The adult who wishes to have a happy relation with his own children or to provide a happy life for them must reflect deeply upon parenthood, and, having reflected, must act wisely. The subject of the family is far too vast to be dealt with in this volume except in relation to our own special problem, namely the conquest of happiness. And even in relation to that problem we can deal with it only in so far as amelioration lies within the power of each individual without alterations in the social structure.

This is, of course, a very grave limitation, for the causes of family unhappiness in our day are of the most diverse sorts, psychological, economic, social, educational, and political. Where the well-to-do sections of the community are concerned, two causes have combined to make women feel parenthood a burden far heavier than it was ever felt to be in former times. These two causes are, on the one hand, the opening of careers to single women; on the other hand, the decay of domestic service. In old days women were driven into marriage by the intolerable conditions of life for the spinster. The spinster had to live at home in economic dependence, first upon her father, and then upon some reluctant brother. She had no occupations to fill her days and no liberty to enjoy herself outside the sheltered walls of the family mansion. She had neither the opportunity nor the inclination for sexual adventure, which she herself profoundly believed to be an abomination except within marriage. If, in spite of all safeguards, she lost her virtue through the wiles of some designing fascinator, her situation was pitiable in the extreme. It is delineated quite accurately in *The Vicar of Wakefield*:

> The only art her guilt to cover,
> To hide her shame from ev'ry eye,
> To give repentance to her lover
> And wring his bosom is—to die.

The modern spinster does not consider death necessary in these circumstances. If she has had a good education, she has no difficulty in making a comfortable living, and is therefore independent of parental approval. Since parents have lost their economic power over their daughters, they have become much more chary of expressing moral disapproval of them; there is not much use in scolding a person who won't stay to be scolded. The unmarried young woman of the professional classes is therefore able nowadays, provided she is not below the average in intelligence and attractiveness, to enjoy a thoroughly agreeable life so long as she can keep free from the desire for children. But if this desire overwhelms her, she is compelled to marry, and almost certainly to lose her job. She sinks to a much lower level of comfort than that to which she has been accustomed, since her husband's income is very likely no larger than that which she was previously earning, and has to provide for a family instead of only a single woman. After having enjoyed independence, she finds it galling to have to look to another for every penny of necessary expenditure. For all these reasons such women hesitate to embark upon maternity.

A woman who nevertheless does take the plunge finds herself, as compared with the women of former generations, confronted with a new and appalling problem, namely the paucity and bad quality of domestic service. In consequence of this, she becomes tied to her house, compelled to perform herself a thousand trivial tasks quite unworthy of her ability and training, or, if she does not perform them herself, to ruin her temper by scolding the maids who neglect them. In regard to the physical care of her children, if she has taken pains to become well-informed in this matter, she finds that it is impossible, without grave risk of disaster, to entrust the children to nurses, or even to leave to others the most elementary precautions in regard to cleanliness and hygiene, unless she can afford a nurse who has had an expensive training at some institute. Weighed down by a mass of trivial detail, she is fortunate indeed if she does not soon lose all her charm and three-quarters of her intelligence. Too often through the mere performance of necessary duties such women become wearisome to their husbands and a nuisance to their children. When the evening comes and her husband returns from his work, the woman who talks about her day-time troubles is a bore, and the woman who does not is absent-minded. In relation to her children, the sacrifices that she has made in order to have them are so present to her mind that she is almost sure to demand more reward than it is desirable to expect, while the constant habit of attending to trivial details will have made her fussy and small-minded. This is the most pernicious of all the injustices that she has to suffer: that in consequence of doing her duty by her family she has lost their affection, whereas if she had neglected them and remained gay and charming they would probably have loved her.[1]

These troubles are essentially economic, and so is another which is almost equally grave. I mean the difficulties in regard to housing which result from the concentration of populations in large cities. In the Middle Ages cities were as rural as the country is now. Children still sing the nursery rhyme:

> Upon Paul's steeple stands a tree
> As full of apples as may be,
> The little boys of London town
> They run with sticks to knock them down.
> And then they run from hedge to hedge
> Until they come to London Bridge.

Paul's steeple is gone, and I do not know at what date the hedges disappeared between St Paul's and London Bridge. It is many

[1] This whole problem as it affects the professional classes is treated with remarkable insight and constructive ability in *The Retreat from Parenthood*, by Jean Ayling.

centuries since the little boys of London town could enjoy such pleasures as this rhyme suggests, but until not so very long ago the bulk of the population lived in the country. The towns were not very vast; it was easy to get out of them, and by no means uncommon to find gardens attached to many houses in them. Nowadays there is in England an immense preponderance of the urban over the rural population. In America this preponderance is as yet slight, but it is very rapidly increasing. Cities like London and New York are so large that it takes a very long time to get out of them. Those who live in the city usually have to be content with a flat, to which, of course, not a square inch of soil is attached, and in which people of moderate means have to be content with the absolute minimum of space. If there are young children, life in a flat is difficult. There is no room for them to play, and there is no room for their parents to get away from their noise. Consequently professional men tend more and more to live in the suburbs. This is undoubtedly desirable from the point of view of the children, but it adds considerably to the fatigue of the man's life, and greatly diminishes the part which he can play in the family.

Such large economic problems, however, it is not my intention to discuss, since they lie outside the problem with which we are concerned, namely what the individual can here and now do to find happiness. We come nearer to this problem when we pass to the psychological difficulties which exist in the present age in the relations of parents and children. These are really part of the problems raised by democracy. In old days there were masters and slaves: the masters decided what was to be done, and on the whole liked their slaves, since their slaves ministered to their happiness. The slaves may possibly have hated their masters, though this did not happen nearly so universally as democratic theory would have us suppose. But even if they did hate their masters, their masters remained unaware of this fact, and the masters at any rate were happy. With the general acceptance of democratic theory all this was changed: slaves who had acquiesced before ceased to acquiesce; masters who had formerly had no doubts as to their rights became hesitant and uncertain. Friction arose and caused unhappiness on both sides. I am not saying all this as an argument against democracy, for the troubles in question are only such as are inevitable in any important transition. But it is no use to blink the fact that, while this transition is in progress, it makes the world uncomfortable.

The change in the relation between parents and children is a particular example of the general spread of democracy. Parents are no longer sure of their rights as against their children; children no longer feel that they owe respect to their parents. The virtue of obedience, which was formerly exacted without question, has become unfashionable, and rightly so. Psycho-analysis has terrified educated parents with the fear of the harm they may unwittingly do their children. If they kiss them, they may produce an Œdipus complex; if they do not they may produce a fury of jealousy. If they order the children to do things they may be producing a sense of sin; if they do not, the children acquire habits which the parents think undesirable. When they see their baby sucking his thumb, they draw all kinds of terrifying inferences, but they are quite at a loss as to what to do to stop him. Parenthood, which used to be a triumphant exercise of power, has become timid, anxious, and filled with conscientious doubts. The old simple joys are lost, and that at the very moment when, owing to the new freedom of single women, the mother has had to sacrifice much more than formerly in deciding upon maternity. In these circumstances conscientious mothers ask too little of their children, and unconscientious mothers ask too much. Conscientious mothers restrain their natural affection and become shy; unconscientious mothers seek in their children a compensation for the joys that they have had to forgo. In the one case the child's affections are starved, in the other they are over-stimulated. In neither case is there any of that simple and natural happiness that the family at its best can provide.

In view of all these troubles, is it any wonder that the birth-rate declines? The decline of the birth-rate in the population at large has reached a point which shows that the population will soon begin to dwindle, but among the well-to-do classes this point has long ago been passed, not only in one country, but in practically all the most highly civilized countries. There are not very many statistics available as to the birth-rate among the well-to-do, but two facts may be quoted from Jean Ayling's book alluded to above.

It appears that in Stockholm in the years 1919 to 1922 the fertility of professional women was only one-third of that of the population at large, and that among the four thousand graduates of Wellesley College, USA, in the period 1896 to 1913 the total number of children is about three thousand, whereas to prevent an actual dwindling of the stock there should have been eight thousand children none of whom had died young. There can be no doubt that the civilization produced by the white races has this singular characteristic, that in proportion as men and women absorb it, they become sterile. The most civilized are the most sterile; the least civilized are the most fertile; and between the two there is a continual gradation. At present the most intelligent sections of the Western nations are dying out. Within a very few years the Western nations as a whole will be diminishing in numbers except in so far as their stocks are replenished by immigration from less civilized regions. And as soon as the immigrants acquire the civilization of the country of their adoption they in turn will become comparatively sterile. It is clear that a civilization which has this characteristic is unstable; unless it can be induced to reproduce its numbers, it must sooner or later die out and give place to some other civilization in which the urge towards parenthood has retained enough strength to prevent the population from declining.

Official moralists in every Western country have endeavoured to treat this problem by means of exhortations and sentimentality. On the one hand, they say that it is the duty of every married couple to have as many children as God wills, regardless of any prospect that such children may have of health and happiness. On the other hand, male divines prate about the sacred joys of motherhood and pretend that a large family of diseased and poverty-stricken infants is a source of happiness. The State joins in with the argument that an adequate crop of cannon fodder is necessary, for how can all these exquisite and ingenious weapons of destruction function adequately unless there are sufficient populations left for them to destroy? Strange to say, the individual parent, even if he accepts these arguments as applied to others, remains entirely deaf to them as applied to himself. The psychology of the divines and the patriots is at fault. The divines may succeed so long as they can successfully threaten hell-fire, but it is only a minority of the population that now takes this threat seriously. And no threat short of this is adequate to control behaviour in a matter so essentially private. As for the State, its argument is altogether too ferocious. People may agree that others ought to provide cannon fodder, but they are not attracted by the prospect of having their own children used in this way. All that the State can do, therefore, is to endeavour to keep the poor in ignorance, an effort which, as the statistics show, is singularly unsuccessful except in the most backward of Western countries. Very few men or women will have children from a sense of public duty, even if it were far clearer than it is that any such public duty exists. When men and women have children, they do so either because they believe that children will add to their happiness, or because they do not know how to prevent them. The latter reason still operates very powerfully, but it is steadily diminishing in potency. And nothing that either the State or the Churches can do will prevent this diminution from continuing. It is necessary, therefore, if the white races are to survive, that parenthood should again become capable of yielding happiness to parents.

When one considers human nature apart from the circumstances of the present day, it is clear, I think, that parenthood is psychologically capable of providing the greatest and most enduring happiness that life has to offer. This, no doubt, is more true of women than of men, but it is more true of men than most moderns are inclined to suppose. It is taken for granted in almost all literature before the present age. Hecuba cares more for her children than for Priam; MacDuff cares more for his children than for his wife. In the Old Testament both men and women are passionately concerned to leave descendants; in China and Japan this attitude has persisted down to our own day. It will be said that this desire is due to ancestor worship. I think, however, that the contrary is the truth, namely that ancestor worship is a reflection of the interest people take in the persistence of their family. Reverting to the professional women whom we were considering a moment ago, it is clear that the urge to have children must be very powerful, for otherwise none of them would make the sacrifices required in order to satisfy it. For my own part, speaking personally, I have found the happiness of parenthood greater than any other that I have experienced. I believe that when circumstances lead men or women to forgo this happiness, a very deep need remains ungratified, and that this produces a dissatisfaction and listlessness of which the cause may remain quite unknown. To be happy in this world, especially when youth is past, it is necessary to feel oneself not merely an isolated individual whose day will soon be over, but part of the stream of life flowing on from the first germ to the remote and unknown future. As a conscious sentiment, expressed in set terms, this involves no doubt a hyper-civilized and intellectual outlook upon the world, but as a vague instinctive emotion it is primitive and natural, and it is its absence that is hyper-civilized. A man who is capable of some great and remarkable achievement which sets its stamp upon future ages may gratify this feeling through his work, but for men and women who have no exceptional gifts, the only way to do so is through children. Those who have allowed their procreative impulses to become atrophied have separated themselves from the stream of life, and in so doing have run a grave risk of becoming desiccated. For them, unless they are exceptionally impersonal, death ends all. The world that shall come after them does not concern them, and because of this their doings appear to themselves trivial and unimportant. To the man or woman who has children and grandchildren and loves them with a natural affection, the future is important, at any rate to the limit of their lives, not only through morality or through an effort of imagination, but naturally and instinctively. And the man whose interests have been stretched to this extent beyond his personal life is likely to be able to stretch them still further. Like Abraham, he will derive satisfaction from the thought that his seed are to inherit the promised land even if this is not to happen for many generations. And through such feelings he is saved from the sense of futility which otherwise deadens all his emotions.

The basis of the family is, of course, the fact that parents feel a special kind of affection towards their own children, different from that which they feel towards each other or towards other children. It is true that some parents feel little or no parental affection, and it is also true that some women are capable of feeling an affection for children not their own almost as strong as that which they could feel for their own. Nevertheless, the broad fact remains that parental affection is a special kind of feeling which the normal human being experiences towards his or her own children, but not towards any other human being. This emotion is one which we inherit from our animal ancestors. In this respect Freud seems to me not sufficiently biological in his outlook, for anyone who will observe an animal mother with her young can see that her behaviour towards them follows an entirely different pattern from her behaviour towards the male with whom she has sex relations. And this same different and instinctive pattern, though in a modified and less definite form, exists among human beings. If it were not for this special emotion there would be almost nothing to be said for the family as an institution, since children might equally well be left to the care of professionals. As things are, however, the special affection which parents have for children, provided their instincts are not atrophied, is of value both to the parents themselves and to the children. The value of parental affection to children lies largely in the fact that it is more reliable than any other affection. One's friends like one for one's merits, one's lovers for one's charms; if the merits or the charms diminish, friends and lovers may vanish. But it is in times of misfortune that parents are most to be relied upon, in illness, and even in disgrace if the parents are of the right sort. We all feel pleasure when we are admired for our merits, but most of us are sufficiently modest at heart to feel that such admiration is precarious. Our parents love us because we are their children, and this is an unalterable fact, so that we feel more safe with them than with anyone else. In times of success this may seem unimportant, but in times of failure it affords a consolation and a security not to be found elsewhere.

In all human relations it is fairly easy to secure happiness for one party, but much more difficult to secure it for both. The gaoler may enjoy guarding the prisoner; the employer may enjoy browbeating the employee; the ruler may enjoy governing his subjects with a firm hand; and the old-fashioned father no doubt enjoyed instilling virtue into his son by means of the rod. These, however, are one-sided pleasures; to the other party in the transaction the situation is less agreeable. We have come to feel that there is something unsatisfactory about these one-sided delights: we believe that a good human relation should be satisfying to both parties. This applies more particularly to the relations of parents and children, with the result that parents obtain far less pleasure from children than they did formerly, while children reciprocally suffer less at the hands of their parents than they did in bygone generations. I do not think there is any real reason why parents should derive less happiness from their children than they did in former times, although undoubtedly this is the case at present. Nor do I think that there is any reason why parents should fail to increase the happiness of their children. But this requires, as do all those equal relationships at which the modern world aims, a certain delicacy and tenderness, a certain reverence for another personality, which are by no means encouraged by the pugnacity of ordinary life. Let us consider the happiness of parenthood, first in its biological essence, and then as it may become in a parent inspired by that kind of attitude towards other personalities which we have been suggesting as essential to a world that believes in equality.

The primitive root of the pleasure of parenthood is two-fold. On the one hand there is the feeling of part of one's own body externalized, prolonging its life beyond the death of the rest of one's body, and possibly in its turn externalizing part of itself in the same fashion, and so securing the immortality of the germ-plasm. On the other hand there is an intimate blend of power and tenderness. The new creature is helpless, and there is an impulse to supply its needs, an impulse which gratifies not only the parent's love towards the child, but also the parent's desire for power. So long as the infant is felt to be helpless, the affection which is bestowed upon it does not feel unselfish, since it is in the nature of protection to a vulnerable portion of oneself. But from a very early age there comes to be a conflict between love of parental power and desire for the child's good, for, while power over the child is to a certain extent decreed by the nature of things, it is nevertheless desirable that the child should as soon as possible learn to be independent in as many ways as possible, which is unpleasant to the power impulse in a parent. Some parents never become conscious of this conflict, and remain tyrants until the children are in a position to rebel. Others, however, become conscious of it, and thus find themselves a prey to conflicting emotions. In this conflict their parental happiness is lost. After all the care that they have bestowed on the child, they find to their mortification that he turns out quite different from what they had hoped. They wanted him to be a soldier, and they find him a pacifist, or, like Tolstoy, they wanted him to be a pacifist, and he joins the Black Hundreds. But it is not only in these later developments that the difficulty is felt. If you feed an infant who is already capable of feeding himself, you are putting love of power before the child's welfare, although it seems to you that you are only being kind in saving him trouble. If you make him too vividly aware of dangers, you are probably actuated by a desire to keep him dependent upon you. If you give him demonstrative affection to which you expect a response, you are probably endeavouring to grapple him to you by means of his emotions. In a thousand ways, great and small, the possessive impulse of parents will lead them astray, unless they are very watchful or very pure in heart. Modern parents, aware of these dangers, sometimes lose confidence in handling their children, and become therefore even less able to be of use to them than if they permitted themselves spontaneous mistakes, for nothing causes so much worry in a child's mind as lack of certainty and self-confidence on the part of an adult. Better than being careful, therefore, is to be pure in heart. The parent who genuinely desires the child's welfare more than his or her power over the child will not need textbooks on psycho-analysis to say what should and what should not be done, but will be guided aright by impulse. And in that case the relation of parent and child will be harmonious from first to last, causing no rebellion in the child and no feeling of frustration in the parent. But this demands on the part of the parent from the first a respect for the personality of the child—a respect which must be not merely a matter of principle, whether moral or intellectual, but something deeply felt with almost mystical conviction to such a degree that possessiveness and oppression become utterly impossible. It is of course not only towards children that an attitude of this sort is desirable: it is very necessary in marriage, and in friendship also, though in friendship it is less difficult. In a good world it would pervade the political relations between groups of human beings, though this is so distant a hope that we need not linger over it. But universal as is the need for this kind of gentleness, it is needed most of all where children are concerned, because of their helplessness, and because their small size and feeble strength cause vulgar souls to despise them.

But to return to the problems with which this book is concerned, the full joy of parenthood in the modern world is only to be obtained by those who can deeply feel this attitude of respect towards the child of which I have been speaking. For to them there will be no irksome restraint upon their love of power, and no need to dread the bitter disillusionment which despotic parents experience when their children acquire freedom. And to the parent who has this attitude there is more joy in parenthood than ever was possible to the despot in the hey-day of parental power. For the love that has been purged by gentleness of all tendency towards tyranny can give a joy more exquisite, more tender, more capable of transmuting the base metal of daily life into the pure gold of mystic ecstasy, than any emotion that is possible to the man still fighting and struggling to maintain his ascendancy in this slippery world.

While I attach a very high value to the parental emotion, I do not draw the inference, which is too commonly drawn, that mothers should do as much as possible themselves for their children. There is a convention on this subject which was all very well in the days when nothing was known about the care of children except the unscientific odds and ends that old women handed on to younger ones. Nowadays there is a great deal in the care of children which is best done by those who have made a special study of some department of this subject. In relation to that part of their education which is *called* 'education' this is recognized. A mother is not expected to teach her son the calculus, however much she may love him. So far as the acquisition of book-learning is concerned, it is recognized that children can acquire it better from those who have it than from a mother who does not have it. But in regard to many other departments in the care of children this is not recognized, because the experience required is not yet recognized. Undoubtedly certain things are better done by the mother, but as the child gets older, there will be an increasing number of things better done by someone else. If this were generally recognized, mothers would be saved a great deal of labour which is irksome to them, because it is not that in which they have professional competence. A woman who has acquired any kind of professional skill ought, both for her own sake and for that of the community, to be free to continue to exercise this skill in spite of motherhood. She may be unable to do so during the later months of pregnancy and during lactation, but a child over nine months old ought not to form an insuperable barrier to its mother's professional activities. Whenever society demands of a mother sacrifices to her child which go beyond reason, the mother, if she is not unusually saintly, will expect from her child compensations exceeding those she has a right to expect. The mother who is conventionally called self-sacrificing is, in a great majority of cases, exceptionally selfish towards her children, for, important as parenthood is as an element in life, it is not satisfying if it is treated as the whole of life, and the unsatisfied parent is likely to be an emotionally grasping parent. It is important, therefore, quite as much in the interests of the children as in those of the mother, that motherhood should not cut her off from all other interests and pursuits. If she has a real vocation for the care of children and that amount of knowledge which will enable her to care adequately for her own children, her skill ought to be more widely used, and she ought to be engaged professionally in the care of some group of children which may be expected to include her own. It is right that parents, provided they fulfil the minimum requirements insisted upon by the State, should have a say as to how their children are cared for and by whom, so long as they do not go outside the ranks of qualified persons. But there should be no convention demanding that every mother should do herself what some other woman can do better. Mothers who feel baffled and incompetent when faced with their children as many mothers do, should have no hesitation in having their children cared for by women who have an aptitude for this work and have undergone the necessary training. There is no heaven-sent instinct which teaches women the right thing to do by their children, and solicitude when it goes beyond a point is a camouflage for possessiveness. Many a child is psychologically ruined by ignorant and sentimental handling on the part of its mother. It has always been recognized that fathers cannot be expected to do very much for their children, and yet children are quite as apt to love their fathers as to love their mothers. The relation of the mother to the child will have in future to resemble more and more that which at present the father has, if women's lives are to be freed from unnecessary slavery and children are to be allowed to profit by the scientific knowledge which is accumulating as to the care of their minds and bodies in early years.

CHAPTER XIV

Work

WHETHER work should be placed among the causes of happiness or among the causes of unhappiness may perhaps be regarded as a doubtful question. There is certainly much work which is exceedingly irksome, and an excess of work is always very painful. I think, however, that, provided work is not excessive in amount, even the dullest work is to most people less painful than idleness. There are in work all grades, from mere relief of tedium up to the profoundest delights, according to the nature of the work and the abilities of the worker. Most of the work that most people have to do is not in itself interesting, but even such work has certain great advantages. To begin with, it fills a good many hours of the day without the need of deciding what one shall do. Most people, when they are left free to fill their own time according to their own choice are at a loss to think of anything sufficiently pleasant to be worth doing. And whatever they decide on, they are troubled by the feeling that something else would have been pleasanter. To be able to fill leisure intelligently is the last product of civilization, and at present very few people have reached this level. Moreover, the exercise of choice is in itself tiresome. Except to people with unusual initiative it is positively agreeable to be told what to do at each hour of the day, provided the orders are not too unpleasant. Most of the idle rich suffer unspeakable boredom as the price of their freedom from drudgery. At times they may find relief by hunting big game in Africa, or by flying round the world, but the number of such sensations is limited, especially after youth is past. Accordingly, the more intelligent rich men work nearly as hard as if they were poor, while rich women for the most part keep themselves busy with innumerable trifles of whose earth-shaking importance they are firmly persuaded.

Work, therefore, is desirable, first and foremost, as a preventive of boredom, for the boredom that a man feels when he is doing necessary though uninteresting work is as nothing in comparison with the boredom that he feels when he has nothing to do with his days. With this advantage of work another is associated, namely that it makes holidays much more delicious when they come. Provided a man does not have to work so hard as to impair his vigour, he is likely to find far more zest in his free time than an idle man could possibly find.

The second advantage of most paid work and of some unpaid work is that it gives chances of success and opportunities for ambition. In most work success is measured by income, and while our capitalistic society continues, this is inevitable. It is only where the best work is concerned that this measure ceases to be the natural one to apply. The desire that men feel to increase their income is quite as much a desire for success as for the extra comforts that a higher income can procure. However dull work may be, it becomes bearable if it is a means of building up a reputation, whether in the world at large or only in one's own circle. Continuity of purpose is one of the most essential ingredients of happiness in the long run, and for most men this comes chiefly through their work. In this respect those women whose lives are occupied with housework are much less fortunate than men, or than women who work outside the home. The domesticated wife does not receive wages, has no means of bettering herself, is taken for granted by her husabnd (who sees practically nothing of what she does), and is valued by him not for her housework but for quite other qualities. Of course, this does not apply to those women who are sufficiently well-to-do to make beautiful houses and beautiful gardens and become the envy of their neighbours; but such women are comparatively few, and for the great majority housework cannot bring as much satisfaction as work of other kinds brings to men and to professional women.

The satisfaction of killing time and of affording some outlet, however modest, for ambition, belongs to most work, and is sufficient to make even a man whose work is dull happier on the average than a man who has no work at all. But when work is interesting, it is capable of giving satisfaction of a far higher order than mere relief from tedium. The kinds of work in which there is some interest may be arranged in a hierarchy. I shall begin with those which are only mildly interesting and end with those that are worthy to absorb the whole energies of a great man.

Two chief elements make work interesting: first, the exercise of skill, and second, construction.

Every man who has acquired some unusual skill enjoys exercising it until it has become a matter of course, or until he can no longer improve himself. This motive to activity begins in early childhood: a boy who can stand on his head becomes reluctant to stand on his feet. A great deal of work gives the same pleasure that is to be derived from games of skill. The work of a lawyer or a politician must contain in a more delectable form a great deal of the same pleasure that is to be derived from playing bridge. Here, of course, there is not only the exercise of skill but the outwitting of a skilled opponent. Even where this competitive element is absent, however, the performance of difficult feats is agreeable. A man who can do stunts in an aeroplane finds the pleasure so great that for the sake of it he is willing to risk his life. I imagine that an able surgeon, in spite of the painful circumstances in which his work is done, derives satisfaction from the exquisite precision of his operations. The same kind of pleasure, though in a less intense form, is to be derived from a great deal of work of a humbler kind. I have even heard of plumbers who enjoyed their work, though I have never had the good fortune to meet one. All skilled work can be pleasurable, provided the skill required is either variable or capable of indefinite improvement. If these conditions are absent, it will cease to be interesting when a man has acquired his maximum skill. A man who runs three-mile races will cease to find pleasure in this occupation when he passes the age at which he can beat his own previous record. Fortunately there is a very considerable amount of work in which new circumstances call for new skill and a man can go on improving, at any rate until he has reached middle age. In some kinds of skilled work, such as politics, for example, it seems that men are at their best between sixty and seventy, the reason being that in such occupations a wide experience of other men is essential. For this reason successful politicians are apt to be happier at the age of seventy than any other men of equal age. Their only competitors in this respect are the men who are the heads of big businesses.

There is, however, another element possessed by the best work, which is even more important as a source of happiness than is the exercise of skill. This is the element of constructiveness. In some work, though by no means in most, something is built up which remains as a monument when the work is completed. We may distinguish construction from destruction by the following criterion. In construction the initial state of affairs is comparatively haphazard, while the final state of affairs embodies a purpose; in destruction the reverse is the case: the initial state of affairs embodies a purpose, while the final state of affairs is haphazard, that is to say, all that is intended by the destroyer is to produce a state of affairs which does not embody a certain purpose. This criterion applies in the most literal and obvious case, namely the construction and destruction of buildings. In constructing a building a previously made plan is carried out, whereas in destroying it no one decides exactly how the materials are to lie when the demolition is complete. Destruction is of course necessary very often as a preliminary to subsequent construction; in that case it is part of a whole which is constructive. But not infrequently a man will engage in activities of which the purpose is destructive without regard to any construction that may come after. Frequently he will conceal this from himself by the belief that he is only sweeping away in order to build afresh, but it is generally possible to unmask this pretence, when it is a pretence, by asking him what the subsequent construction is to be. On this subject it will be found that he will speak vaguely and without enthusiasm, whereas on the preliminary destruction he has spoken precisely and with zest. This applies to not a few revolutionaries and militarists and other apostles of violence. They are actuated, usually without their own knowledge, by hatred; the destruction of what they hate is their real purpose, and they are comparatively indifferent to the question what is to come after it. Now I cannot deny that in the work of destruction as in the work of construction there may be joy. It is a fiercer joy, perhaps at moments more intense, but it is less profoundly satisfying, since the result is one in which little satisfaction is to be found. You kill your enemy, and when he is dead your occupation is gone, and the satisfaction that you derive from victory quickly fades. The work of construction, on the other hand, when completed, is delightful to contemplate, and moreover is never so fully completed that there is nothing further to do about it. The most satisfactory purposes are those that lead on indefinitely from one success to another without ever coming to a dead end; and in this respect it will be found that construction is a greater source of happiness than destruction. Perhaps it would be more correct to say that those who find satisfaction in construction find in it greater satisfaction than the lovers of destruction can find in destruction, for if once you have become filled with hate you will not easily derive from construction the pleasure which another man would derive from it.

At the same time few things are so likely to cure the habit of hatred as the opportunity to do constructive work of an important kind.

The satisfaction to be derived from success in a great constructive enterprise is one of the most massive that life has to offer, although unfortunately in its highest forms it is only open to men of exceptional ability. Nothing can rob a man of the happiness of successful achievement in an important piece of work, unless it be the proof that after all his work was bad. There are many forms of such satisfaction. The man who by a scheme of irrigation has caused the wilderness to blossom like the rose enjoys it in one of its most tangible forms. The creation of an organization may be a work of supreme importance. So is the work of those few statesmen who have devoted their lives to producing order out of chaos, of whom Lenin is the supreme type in our day. The most obvious examples are artists and men of science. Shakespeare says of his verse: 'So long as men can breathe, or eyes can see, so long lives this.' And it cannot be doubted that the thought consoled him for misfortune. In his sonnets he maintains that the thought of his friend reconciled him to life, but I cannot help suspecting that the sonnets he wrote to his friend were even more effective for this purpose than the friend himself. Great artists and great men of science do work which is in itself delightful; while they are doing it, it secures them the respect of those whose respect is worth having, which gives them the most fundamental kind of power, namely power over men's thoughts and feelings. They have also the most solid reasons for thinking well of themselves. This combination of fortunate circumstances ought, one would think, to be enough to make any man happy. Nevertheless it is not so. Michael Angelo, for example, was a profoundly unhappy man and maintained (not, I am sure, with truth) that he would not have troubled to produce works of art if he had not had to pay the debts of his impecunious relations. The power to produce great art is very often, though by no means always, associated with a temperamental unhappiness, so great that but for the joy which the artist derives from his work he would be driven to suicide. We cannot therefore maintain that even the greatest work must make a man happy; we can only maintain that it must make him less unhappy. Men of science, however, are far less often temperamentally unhappy than artists are, and in the main the men who do great work in science are happy men, whose happiness is derived primarily from their work.

One of the causes of unhappiness among intellectuals in the present day is that so many of them, especially those whose skill is literary, find no opportunity for the independent exercise of their talents, but have to hire themselves out to rich corporations directed by Philistines, who insist upon their producing what they themselves regard as pernicious nonsense. If you were to inquire among journalists either in England or America whether they believed in the policy of the newspaper for which they worked, you would find, I believe, that only a small minority do so; the rest, for the sake of a livelihood, prostitute their skill to purposes which they believe to be harmful. Such work cannot bring any real satisfaction, and in the course of reconciling himself to the doing of it a man has to make himself so cynical that he can no longer derive whole-hearted satisfaction from anything whatever. I cannot condemn men who undertake work of this sort, since starvation is too serious an alternative, but I think that where it is possible to do work that is satisfactory to a man's constructive impulses without entirely starving, he will be well advised from the point of view of his own happiness if he chooses it in preference to work much more highly paid but not seeming to him worth doing on its own account. Without self-respect genuine happiness is scarcely possible. And the man who is ashamed of his work can hardly achieve self-respect.

The satisfaction of constructive work, though it may, as things are, be the privilege of a minority, can nevertheless be the privilege of a quite large minority. Any man who is his own master in his work can feel it; so can any man whose work appears to him useful and requires considerable skill. The production of satisfactory children is a difficult constructive work capable of affording profound satisfaction. Any woman who has achieved this can feel that as a result of her labour the world contains something of value which is would not otherwise contain.

Human beings differ profoundly in regard to the tendency to regard their lives as a whole. To some men it is natural to do so, and essential to happiness to be able to do so with some satisfaction. To others life is a series of detached incidents without directed movement and without unity. I think the former sort are more likely to achieve happiness than the latter, since they will gradually build up those circumstances from which they can derive contentment and self-respect, whereas the others will be blown about by the winds of circumstance now this way, now that, without ever arriving at any haven. The habit of viewing life as a whole is an essential part both of wisdom and of true morality, and is one of the things which ought to be encouraged in education. Consistent purpose is not enough to make life happy, but it is an almost indispensable condition of a happy life. And consistent purpose embodies itself mainly in work.

CHAPTER XV

Impersonal Interests

In this chapter I wish to consider not those major interests about which a man's life is built, but those minor interests which fill his leisure and afford relaxation from the tenseness of his more serious pre-occupations. In the life of the average man his wife and children, his work and his financial position occupy the main part of his anxious and serious thought. Even if he has extra-matrimonial love affairs, they probably do not concern him as profoundly in themselves as in their possible effects upon his home life. The interests which are bound up with his work I am not for the present regarding as impersonal interests. A man of science, for example, must keep abreast of research in his own line. Towards such research his feelings have the warmth and vividness belonging to something intimately concerned with his career, but if he reads about research in some quite other science with which he is not professionally concerned he reads in quite a different spirit, not professionally, less critically, more disinterestedly. Even if he has to use his mind in order to follow what is said, his reading is nevertheless a relaxation, because it is not connected with his responsibilities. If the book interests him, his interest is impersonal in a sense which cannot be applied to the books upon his own subject. It is such interests lying outside the main activities of a man's life that I wish to speak about in the present chapter.

One of the sources of unhappiness, fatigue, and nervous strain is inability to be interested in anything that is not of practical importance in one's own life. The result of this is that the conscious mind gets no rest from a certain small number of matters, each of which probably involves some anxiety and some element of worry. Except in sleep the conscious mind is never allowed to lie fallow while subconscious thought matures its gradual wisdom. The result is excitability, lack of sagacity, irritability, and a loss of sense of proportion. All these are both causes and effects of fatigue.

As a man gets more tired, his external interests fade, and as they fade he loses the relief which they afford him and becomes still more tired. This vicious circle is only too apt to end in a breakdown. What is restful about external interests is the fact that they do not call for any action. Making decisions and exercising volition are very fatiguing, especially if they have to be done hurriedly and without the help of the subconscious. Men who feel that they must 'sleep on it' before coming to an important decision are profoundly right. But it is not only in sleep that the subconscious mental processes can work. They can work also while a man's conscious mind is occupied elsewhere. The man who can forget his work when it is over and not remember it until it begins again next day is likely to do his work far better than the man who worries about it throughout the intervening hours. And it is very much easier to forget work at the times when it ought to be forgotten if a man has many interests other than his work than it is if he has not. It is, however, essential that these interests should not exercise those very faculties which have been exhausted by his day's work. They should not involve will and quick decision, they should not, like gambling, involve any financial element, and they should as a rule not be so exciting as to produce emotional fatigue and preoccupy the subconscious as well as the conscious mind.

A great many amusements fulfil all these conditions. Watching games, going to the theatre, playing golf, are all irreproachable from this point of view. For a man of a bookish turn of mind reading unconnected with his professional activities is very satisfactory. However important a worry may be, it should not be thought about throughout the whole of the waking hours.

In this respect there is a great difference between men and women. Men on the whole find it very much easier to forget their work than women do. In the case of women whose work is in the home this is natural, since they do not have the change of place that a man has when he leaves the office to help them to acquire a new mood. But if I am not mistaken, women whose work is outside the home differ from men in this respect almost as much as those who work at home. They find it, that is to say, very difficult to be interested in anything that has for them no practical importance. Their purposes govern their thoughts and their activities, and they seldom become absorbed in some wholly irresponsible interest. I do not of course deny that exceptions exist, but I am speaking of what seems to me to be the usual rule. In a woman's college, for example, the women teachers, if no man is present, talk shop in the evening, while in a man's college the men do not. This characteristic appears to women as a higher degree of conscientiousness than that of men, but I do not think that in the long run it improves the quality of their work. And it tends to produce a certain narrowness of outlook leading not infrequently to a kind of fanaticism.

All impersonal interests, apart from their importance as relaxation, have various other uses. To begin with, they help a man to retain his sense of proportion. It is very easy to become so absorbed in our own pursuits, our own circle, our own type of work, that we forget how small a part this is of the total of human activity and how many things in the world are entirely unaffected by what we do. Why should one remember this? you may ask. There are several answers. In the first place, it is good to have as true a picture of the world as is compatible with necessary activities. Each of us is in the world for no very long time, and within the few years of his life has to acquire whatever he is to know of this strange planet and its place in the universe. To ignore our opportunities for knowledge, imperfect as they are, is like going to the theatre and not listening to the play. The world is full of things that are tragic or comic, heroic or bizarre or surprising, and those who fail to be interested in the spectacle that it offers are forgoing one of the privileges that life has to offer.

Then again a sense of proportion is very valuable and at times very consoling. We are all inclined to get unduly excited, unduly strained, unduly impressed with the importance of the little corner of the world in which we live, and of the little moment of time comprised between our birth and death. In this excitement and over-estimation of our own importance there is nothing desirable. True, it may make us work harder, but it will not make us work better. A little work directed to a good end is better than a great deal of work directed to a bad end, though the apostles of the strenuous life seem to think otherwise. Those who care much for their work are always in danger of falling into fanaticism, which consists essentially in remembering one or two desirable things while forgetting all the rest, and in supposing that in the pursuit of these one or two any incidental harm of other sorts is of little account. Against this fanatical temper there is no better prophylactic than a large conception of the life of man and his place in the universe. This may seem a very big thing to invoke in such a connection, but apart from this particular use it is in itself a thing of great value.

It is one of the defects of modern higher education that it has become too much a training in the acquisition of certain kinds of skill, and too little an enlargement of the mind and heart by an impartial survey of the world. You become absorbed, let us say, in a political contest, and work hard for the victory of your own party. So far, so good. But it may happen in the course of the contest that some opportunity of victory presents itself which involves the use of methods calculated to increase hatred, violence and suspicion in the world. For example, you may find that the best road to victory is to insult some foreign nation. If your mental purview is limited to the present, or if you have imbibed the doctrine that what is called efficiency is the only thing that matters, you will adopt such dubious means. Through them you will be victorious in your immediate purpose, while the more distant consequences may be disastrous. If, on the other hand, you have as part of the habitual furniture of your mind the past ages of man, his slow and partial emergence out of barbarism, and the brevity of his total existence in comparison with astronomical epochs—if, I say, such thoughts have moulded your habitual feelings, you will realize that the momentary battle upon which you are engaged cannot be of such importance as to risk a backward step towards the darkness out of which we have been slowly emerging. Nay, more, if you suffer defeat in your immediate objective, you will be sustained by the same sense of its momentariness that made you unwilling to adopt degrading weapons. You will have, beyond your immediate activities, purposes that are distant and slowly unfolding, in which you are not an isolated individual but one of the great army of those who have led mankind towards a civilized existence. If you have attained to this outlook, a certain deep happiness will never leave you, whatever your personal fate may be. Life will become a communion with the great of all ages, and personal death no more than a negligible incident.

If I had the power to organize higher education as I should wish it to be, I should seek to substitute for the old orthodox religions —which appeal to few among the young, and those as a rule the least intelligent and the most obscurantist—something which is perhaps hardly to be called religion, since it is merely a focusing of attention upon well-ascertained facts. I should seek to make young people vividly aware of the past, vividly realizing that the future of man will in all likelihood be immeasurably longer than his past, profoundly conscious of the minuteness of the planet upon which we live and of the fact that life on this planet is only a temporary incident; and at the same time with these facts which tend to emphasize the insignificance of the individual I should present quite another set of facts designed to impress upon the mind of the young the greatness of which the individual is capable, and the knowledge that throughout all the depths of stellar space nothing of equal value is known to us. Spinoza long ago wrote of human bondage and human freedom; his form and his language make his thought difficult of access to all but students of philosophy, but the essence of what I wish to convey differs little from what he has said.

A man who has once perceived, however temporarily and however briefly, what makes greatness of soul, can no longer be happy if he allows himself to be petty, self-seeking, troubled by trivial misfortunes, dreading what fate may have in store for him. The man capable of greatness of soul will open wide the windows of his mind, letting the winds blow freely upon it from every portion of the universe. He will see himself and life and the world as truly as our human limitations will permit; realizing the brevity and minuteness of human life, he will realize also that in individual minds is concentrated whatever of value the known universe contains. And he will see that the man whose mind mirrors the world becomes in a sense as great as the world. In emancipation from the fears that beset the slave of circumstance he will experience a profound joy, and through all the vicissitudes of his outward life he will remain in the depths of his being a happy man.

Leaving these large speculations and returning to our more

immediate subject, namely the value of impersonal interests, there is another consideration which makes them a great help towards happiness. Even in the most fortunate lives there are times when things go wrong. Few men except bachelors have never quarrelled with their wives; few parents have not endured grave anxiety owing to the illnesses of their children; few business men have avoided times of financial stress; few professional men have not known periods when failure stared them in the face. At such times a capacity to become interested in something outside the cause of anxiety is an immense boon. At such times, when in spite of anxiety there is nothing to be done at the moment, one man will play chess, another will read detective stories, a third will become absorbed in popular astronomy, a fourth will console himself by reading about the excavations at Ur of the Chaldees. Any one of these four is acting wisely, whereas the man who does nothing to distract his mind and allows his trouble to acquire a complete empire over him is acting unwisely and making himself less fit to cope with his troubles when the moment for action arrives. Very similar considerations apply to irreparable sorrows such as the death of some person deeply loved. No good is done to anyone by allowing oneself to become sunk in grief on such an occasion. Grief is unavoidable and must be expected, but everything that can be done should be done to minimize it. It is mere sentimentality to aim, as some do, at extracting the very uttermost drop of misery from misfortune. I do not of course deny that a man may be broken by sorrow, but I do say that every man should do his utmost to escape this fate, and should seek any distraction, however trivial, provided it is not in itself harmful or degrading. Among those that I regard as harmful and degrading I include such things as drunkenness and drugs, of which the purpose is to destroy thought, at least for the time being. The proper course is not to destroy thought but to turn it into new channels, or at any rate into channels remote from the present misfortune. It is difficult to do this if life has hitherto been concentrated upon a very few interests and those few have now become suffused with sorrow. To bear misfortune well when it comes, it is wise to have cultivated in happier times a certain width of interests, so that the mind may find prepared for it some undisturbed place suggesting other associations and other emotions than those which are making the present difficult to bear.

A man of adequate vitality and zest will surmount all misfortunes by the emergence after each blow of an interest in life and the world which cannot be narrowed down so much as to make one loss fatal. To be defeated by one loss or even by several is not something to be admired as a proof of sensibility, but something to be deplored as a failure in vitality. All our affections are at the mercy of death, which may strike down those whom we love at any moment. It is therefore necessary that our lives should not have that narrow intensity which puts the whole meaning and purpose of our life at the mercy of accident.

For all these reasons the man who pursues happiness wisely will aim at the possession of a number of subsidiary interests in addition to those central ones upon which his life is built.

CHAPTER XVI

Effort and Resignation

THE golden mean is an uninteresting doctrine, and I can remember when I was young rejecting it with scorn and indignation, since in those days it was heroic extremes that I admired. Truth, however, is not always interesting, and many things are believed because they are interesting although, in fact, there is little other evidence in their favour. The golden mean is a case in point: it may be an uninteresting doctrine, but in a very great many matters it is a true one.

One respect in which it is necessary to preserve the golden mean is as regards the balance between effort and resignation. Both doctrines have had extreme advocates. The doctrine of resignation has been preached by saints and mystics; the doctrine of effort has been preached by efficiency experts and muscular Christians. Each of these opposing schools has had a part of the truth, but not the whole. I want in this chapter to try and strike the balance, and I shall begin with the case in favour of effort.

Happiness is not, except in very rare cases, something that drops into the mouth, like a ripe fruit, by the mere operation of fortunate circumstances. That is why I have called this book *The Conquest of Happiness*. For in a world so full of avoidable and unavoidable misfortunes, of illness and psychological tangles, of struggle and poverty and ill will, the man or woman who is to be happy must find ways of coping with the multitudinous causes of unhappiness by which each individual is assailed. In some rare cases no great effort may be required. A man of easy good nature, who inherits an ample fortune and enjoys good health together with simple tastes, may slip through life comfortably and wonder what all the fuss is about; a good-looking woman of an indolent disposition, if she happens to marry a well-to-do husband who demands no exertion from her, and if after marriage she does not mind growing fat, may equally enjoy a certain lazy comfort, provided she has good luck as regards her children. But such cases are exceptional. Most people are not rich; many people are not born good-natured; many people have uneasy passions which make a quiet and well-regulated life seem intolerably boring; health is a blessing which no one can be sure of preserving; marriage is not invariably a source of bliss. For all these reasons, happiness must be, for most men and women, an achievement rather than a gift of the gods, and in this achievement effort, both inward and outward, must play a great part. The inward effort may include the effort of necessary resignation; for the present, therefore, let us consider only outward effort.

In the case of any person, whether man or woman, who has to work for a living, the need of effort in this respect is too obvious to need emphasizing. The Indian fakir, it is true, can make a living without effort by merely offering a bowl for the alms of the faithful, but in Western countries the authorities do not view with a favourable eye this method of obtaining an income. Moreover, the climate makes it less pleasant than in hotter and drier countries: in the winter-time, at any rate, few people are so lazy as to prefer idleness out of doors to work in heated rooms. Resignation alone, therefore, is not in the West one of the roads to fortune.

To a very large percentage of men in Western countries, more than a bare living is necessary to happiness, since they desire the feeling of being successful. In some occupations, such, for example as scientific research, this feeling can be obtained by men who do not earn a large income, but in the majority of occupations income has become the measure of success. At this point we touch upon a matter in regard to which an element of resignation is desirable in most cases, since in a competitive world conspicuous success is possible only for a minority.

Marriage is a matter in regard to which effort may or may not be necessary, according to circumstances. Where one sex is in the minority, as men are in England and women are in Australia, members of that sex require, as a rule, little effort in order to marry if they wish. For members of the sex which is in the majority, however, the opposite is the case. The amount of effort and thought expended in this direction by women where they are in the majority is obvious to anyone who will study the advertise-

ments in women's magazines. Men, where they are in a majority,
frequently adopt more expeditious methods, such as skill with the
revolver. This is natural, since a majority of men occurs most
frequently on the border-line of civilization. I do not know what
men would do if a discriminating pestilence caused them to
become a majority in England; they might have to revert to the
manners of gallants in a bygone age.

The amount of effort involved in the successful rearing of children is so evident that probably no one would deny it. Countries
which believe in resignation and what is mistakenly called a
'spiritual' view of life are countries with a high infant mortality.
Medicine, hygiene, asepsis, suitable diet, are things not achieved
without mundane preoccupations; they require energy and intelligence directed to the material environment. Those who think
that matter is an illusion are apt to think the same of dirt, and by
so thinking to cause their children to die.

Speaking more generally, one may say that some kind of power
forms the normal and legitimate aim of every person whose
natural desires are not atrophied. The kind of power that a man
desires depends upon his predominant passions; one man desires
power over the actions of men, another desires power over their
thoughts, a third power over their emotions. One man desires to
change the material environment, another desires the sense of
power that comes from intellectual mastery. Every kind of public
work involves desire for some kind of power, unless it is under-
taken solely with a view to the wealth obtainable by corruption.
The man who is actuated by purely altruistic suffering caused by
the spectacle of human misery will, if his suffering is genuine,
desire power to alleviate misery. The only man totally indifferent
to power is the man totally indifferent to his fellow-men. Some
form of desire for power is therefore to be accepted as part of the
equipment of the kind of men out of whom a good community can
be made. And every form of desire for power involves, so long as it
is not thwarted, a correlative form of effort. To the mentality of
the West this conclusion may seem a commonplace, but there
are not a few in Western countries who coquette with what is
called 'the wisdom of the East' just at the moment when the
East is abandoning it. To them perhaps what we have been

saying may appear questionable, and if so, it has been worth saying.

Resignation, however, has also its part to play in the conquest of happiness, and it is a part no less essential than that played by effort. The wise man, though he will not sit down under preventable misfortunes, will not waste time and emotion upon such as are unavoidable, and even such as are in themselves avoidable he will submit to if the time and labour required to avoid them would interfere with the pursuit of some more important object. Many people get into a fret or a fury over every little thing that goes wrong, and in this way waste a great deal of energy that might be more usefully employed. Even in the pursuit of really important objects it is unwise to become so deeply involved emotionally that the thought of possible failure becomes a constant menace to peace of mind. Christianity taught submission to the will of God, and even for those who cannot accept this phraseology there should be something of the same kind pervading all their activities. Efficiency in a practical task is not proportional to the emotion that we put into it; indeed, emotion is sometimes an obstacle to efficiency. The attitude required is that of doing one's best while leaving the issue to fate. Resignation is of two sorts, one rooted in despair, the other in unconquerable hope. The first is bad; the second is good. The man who has suffered such fundamental defeat that he has given up hope of serious achievement may learn the resignation of despair, and, if he does, he will abandon all serious activity. He may camouflage his despair by religious phrases, or by the doctrine that contemplation is the true end of man, but whatever disguise he may adopt to conceal his inward defeat, he will remain essentially useless and fundamentally unhappy. The man whose resignation is based on unconquerable hope acts in quite a different way. Hope which is to be unconquerable must be large and impersonal. Whatever my personal activities, I may be defeated by death, or by certain kinds of diseases; I may be overcome by my enemies; I may find that I have embarked upon an unwise course which cannot lead to success. In a thousand ways the failure of purely personal hopes may be unavoidable, but if personal aims have been part of larger hopes for humanity, there is not the same utter defeat when failure comes. The man of science who desires to make great discoveries himself may fail to do so, or may have to abandon his work owing to a blow on the head, but if he desires profoundly the progress of science and not merely his personal contribution to this object, he will not feel the same despair as would be felt by a man whose research had purely egoistic motives. The man who is working for some much needed reform may find all his efforts sidetracked by a war, and may be forced to realize that what he has worked for will not come about in his lifetime. But he need not on that account sink into complete despair, provided that he is interested in the future of mankind apart from his own participation in it.

The cases we have been considering are those in which resignation is most difficult; there are a number of others in which it is much easier. These are the cases in which only subsidiary purposes suffer a check, while the major purposes of life continue to offer a prospect of success. A man, for example, who is engaged in important work shows a failure in the desirable kind of resignation if he is distracted by matrimonial unhappiness; if his work is really absorbing, he should regard such incidental troubles in the way in which one regards a wet day, that is to say, as a nuisance about which it would be foolish to make a fuss.

Some people are unable to bear with patience even those minor troubles which make up, if we permit them to do so, a very large part of life. They are furious when they miss a train, transported with rage if their dinner is badly cooked, sunk in despair if the chimney smokes, and vowing vengeance against the whole industrial order when their clothes fail to return from the sanitary steam laundry. The energy that such people waste on trivial troubles would be sufficient, it more wisely directed, to make and unmake empires. The wise man fails to observe the dust that the housemaid has not dusted, the potato that the cook has not cooked, and the soot that the sweep has not swept. I do not mean that he takes no steps to remedy these matters, provided he has time to do so; I mean only that he deals with them without emotion. Worry and fret and irritation are emotions which serve no purpose. Those who feel them strongly may say that they are incapable of overcoming them, and I am not sure that they can be overcome by anything short of that fundamental resignation of which we

spoke earlier. The same kind of concentration upon large impersonal hopes which enables a man to bear personal failure in his
work, or the troubles of an unhappy marriage, will also make it
possible for him to be patient when he misses a train or drops his
umbrella in the mud. If he is of a fretful disposition, I am not sure
that anything less than this will cure him.

The man who has become emancipated from the empire of
worry will find life a much more cheerful affair than it used to be
while he was perpetually being irritated. Personal idiosyncracies of
acquaintances, which formerly made him wish to scream, will now
seem merely amusing. When Mr A. for the three hundred and
forty-seventh time relates the anecdote of the Bishop of Tierra del
Fuego, he amuses himself by noting the score, and feels no
inclination to attempt a vain diversion by an anecdote of his own.
When his bootlace breaks just as he is in a hurry to catch an early
morning train, he reflects, after the appropriate expletives, that in
the history of the cosmos the event in question has no very great
importance. When he is interrupted in a proposal of marriage by a
visit of a tedious neighbour, he considers that all mankind have
been liable to disaster, with the exception of Adam, and that even
he had his troubles. There is no limit to what can be done in the
way of finding consolation from minor misfortunes by means of
bizarre analogies and quaint parallels. Every civilized man or
woman has, I suppose, some picture of himself or herself, and is
annoyed when anything happens that seems to spoil this picture.
The best cure is to have not only one picture, but a whole gallery,
and to select the one appropriate to the incident in question. If
some of the portraits are a trifle laughable, so much the better; it
is not wise to see oneself all day long as a hero of high tragedy.
I do not suggest that one should see oneself always as a clown in
comedy, for those who do this are even more irritating; a little
tact is required in choosing a role appropriate to the situation. Of
course, if you can forget yourself and not play a part at all that is
admirable. But if playing a part has become second nature, consider that you act in repertory, and so avoid monotony.

Many active people are of opinion that the slightest grain of
resignation, the faintest gleam of humour, would destroy the
energy with which they do their work and the determination by

which, as they believe, they achieve success. These people, in my opinion, are mistaken. Work that is worth doing can be done even by those who do not deceive themselves either as to its importance or as to the ease with which it can be done. Those who can only do their work when upheld by self-deception had better first take a course in learning to endure the truth before continuing their career, since sooner or later the need of being sustained by myths will cause their work to become harmful instead of beneficial. It is better to do nothing than to do harm. Half the useful work in the world consists of combating the harmful work. A little time spent in learning to appreciate facts is not time wasted, and the work that will be done afterwards is far less likely to be harmful than the work done by those who need a continual inflation of their ego as a stimulant to their energy. A certain kind of resignation is involved in willingness to face the truth about ourselves; this kind, though it may involve pain in the first moments, affords ultimately a protection—indeed the only possible protection—against the disappointments and disillusionments to which the self-deceiver is liable. Nothing is more fatiguing nor, in the long run, more exasperating than the daily effort to believe things which daily become more incredible. To be done with this effort is an indispensable condition of secure and lasting happiness.

CHAPTER XVII

The Happy Man

HAPPINESS, as is evident, depends partly upon external circumstances and partly upon oneself. We have been concerned in this volume with the part which depends upon oneself, and we have been led to the view that so far as this part is concerned the recipe for happiness is a very simple one. It is thought by many, among whom I think we must include Mr Krutch, whom we considered in an earlier chapter, that happiness is impossible without a creed of a more or less religious kind. It is thought by many who are themselves unhappy that their sorrows have complicated and highly intellectualized sources. I do not believe that such things are genuine causes of either happiness or unhappiness; I think they are only symptoms. The man who is unhappy will, as a rule, adopt an unhappy creed, while the man who is happy will adopt a happy creed; each may attribute his happiness or unhappiness to his beliefs, while the real causation is the other way round. Certain things are indispensable to the happiness of most men, but these are simple things: food and shelter, health, love, successful work and the respect of one's own herd. To some people parenthood also is essential. Where these things are lacking, only the exceptional man can achieve happiness, but where they are enjoyed, or can be obtained by well-directed effort, the man who is still unhappy is suffering from some psychological maladjustment which, if it is very grave, may need the services of a psychiatrist, but can in ordinary cases be cured by the patient himself, provided he sets about the matter in the right way. Where outward circumstances are not definitely unfortunate, a man should be able to achieve happiness, provided that his passions and interests are directed outward, not inward. It should be our endeavour therefore, both in education and in attempts to adjust ourselves to the world, to aim at avoiding self-centred passions and at acquiring those affections and those interests which will prevent our thoughts from dwelling perpetually upon ourselves. It is not the nature of most men to be happy in a prison, and the passions which shut us up in ourselves constitute one of the worst kinds of prisons. Among such passions some of the commonest are fear, envy, the sense of sin, self-pity and self-admiration. In all these our desires are centred upon ourselves: there is no genuine interest in the outer world, but only a concern lest it should in some way injure us or fail to feed our ego. Fear is the principal reason why men are so unwilling to admit facts and so anxious to wrap themselves round in a warm garment of myth. But the thorns tear the warm garment and the cold blasts penetrate through the rents, and the man who has become accustomed to its warmth suffers far more from these blasts than a man who has hardened himself to them from the first. Moreover, those who deceive themselves generally know at bottom that they are doing so, and live in a state of apprehension lest some untoward event should force unwelcome realizations upon them.

One of the great drawbacks to self-centred passions is that they afford so little variety in life. The man who loves only himself cannot, it is true, be accused of promiscuity in his affections, but he is bound in the end to suffer intolerable boredom from the invariable sameness of the object of his devotion. The man who suffers from a sense of sin is suffering from a particular kind of self-love. In all this vast universe the thing that appears to him of most importance is that he himself should be virtuous. It is a grave defect in certain forms of traditional religion that they have encouraged this particular kind of self-absorption.

The happy man is the man who lives objectively, who has free affections and wide interests, who secures his happiness through these interests and affections and through the fact that they, in turn, make him an object of interest and affection to many others. To be the recipient of affection is a potent cause of happiness, but the man who demands affection is not the man upon whom it is bestowed. The man who receives affection is, speaking broadly, the man who gives it. But it is useless to attempt to give it as a calculation, in the way in which one might lend money at interest, for a calculated affection is not genuine and is not felt to be so by the recipient.

What then can a man do who is unhappy because he is encased

in self? So long as he continues to think about the causes of his unhappiness, he continues to be self-centred and therefore does not get outside the vicious circle; if he is to get outside it, it must be by genuine interests, not by simulated interests adopted merely as a medicine. Although this difficulty is real, there is nevertheless much that he can do if he has rightly diagnosed his trouble. If, for example, his trouble is due to a sense of sin, conscious or unconscious, he can first persuade his conscious mind that he has no reason to feel sinful, and then proceed, by the kind of technique that we have considered in earlier chapters, to plant this rational conviction in his unconscious mind, concerning himself meanwhile with some more or less neutral activity. If he succeeds in dispelling the sense of sin, it is probable that genuinely objective interests will arise spontaneously. If his trouble is self-pity, he can deal with it in the same manner after first persuading himself that there is nothing extraordinarily unfortunate in his circumstances. If fear is his trouble, let him practise exercises designed to give courage. Courage in war has been recognized from time immemorial as an important virtue, and a great part of the training of boys and young men has been devoted to producing a type of character capable of fearlessness in battle. But moral courage and intellectual courage have been much less studied; they also, however, have their technique. Admit to yourself every day at least one painful truth; you will find this quite as useful as the Boy Scout's daily kind action. Teach yourself to feel that life would still be worth living even if you were not, as of course you are, immeasurably superior to all your friends in virtue and in intelligence. Exercises of this sort prolonged through several years will at last enable you to admit facts without flinching, and will, in so doing, free you from the empire of fear over a very large field.

What the objective interests are to be that will arise in you when you have overcome the disease of self-absorption must be left to the spontaneous workings of your nature and of external circumstances. Do not say to yourself in advance, 'I should be happy if I could become absorbed in stamp-collecting', and thereupon set to work to collect stamps, for it may well happen that you will fail altogether to find stamp-collecting interesting. Only what genuinely interests you can be of any use to you, but you may be pretty sure that genuine objective interests will grow up as soon as you have learnt not to be immersed in self.

The happy life is to an extraordinary extent the same as the good life. Professional moralists have made too much of self-denial, and in so doing have put the emphasis in the wrong place. Conscious self-denial leaves a man self-absorbed and vividly aware of what he has sacrificed; in consequence it fails often of its immediate object and almost always of its ultimate purpose. What is needed is not self-denial, but that kind of direction of interest outward which will lead spontaneously and naturally to the same acts that a person absorbed in the pursuit of his own virtue could only perform by means of conscious self-denial. I have written in this book as a hedonist, that is to say, as one who regards happiness as the good, but the acts to be recommended from the point of view of the hedonist are on the whole the same as those to be recommended by the sane moralist. The moralist, however, is too apt, though this is not, of course, universally true, to stress the act rather than the state of mind. The effects of an act upon the agent will be widely different, according to his state of mind at the moment. If you see a child drowning and save it as the result of a direct impulse to bring help, you will emerge none the worse morally. If, on the other hand, you say to yourself, 'It is the part of virtue to succour the helpless, and I wish to be a virtuous man, therefore I must save this child', you will be an even worse man afterwards than you were before. What applies in this extreme case applies in many other instances that are less obvious.

There is another difference, somewhat more subtle, between the attitude towards life that I have been recommending and that which is recommended by the traditional moralists. The traditional moralist, for example, will say that love should be unselfish. In a certain sense he is right, that is to say, it should not be selfish beyond a point, but it should undoubtedly be of such a nature that one's own happiness is bound up in its success. If a man were to invite a lady to marry him on the ground that he ardently desired her happiness and at the same time considered that she would afford him ideal opportunities of self-abnegation, I think it may be doubted whether she would be altogether pleased. Undoubtedly we should desire the happiness of those whom we love, but not as an alternative to our own. In fact the whole antithesis between self and the rest of the world, which is implied in the doctrine of self-denial, disappears as soon as we have any genuine interest in persons or things outside ourselves. Through such interests a man comes to feel himself part of the stream of life, not a hard separate entity like a billiard-ball, which can have no relation with other such entities except that of collision. All unhappiness depends upon some kind of disintegration or lack of integration; there is disintegration within the self through lack of co-ordination between the conscious and the unconscious mind; there is lack of integration between the self and society where the two are not knit together by the force of objective interests and affections. The happy man is the man who does not suffer from either of these failures of unity, whose personality is neither divided against itself nor pitted against the world. Such a man feels himself a citizen of the universe, enjoying freely the spectacle that it offers and the joys that it affords, untroubled by the thought of death because he feels himself not really separate from those who will come after him. It is in such profound instinctive union with the stream of life that the greatest joy is to be found.

GEORGE ALLEN & UNWIN LTD

Head office:
40 Museum Street, London, W.C.1
Telephone: 01-405 8577

Sales, Distribution and Accounts Departments
Park Lane, Hemel Hempstead, Herts.
Telephone: 0442 3244

Athens: 7 Stadiou Street, Athens 125
Barbados: Rockley New Road, St. Lawerence 4
Bombay: 103/5 Fort Street, Bombay 1
Calcutta: 285J Bepin Behari Ganguli Street, Calcutta 12
Dacca: Alico Building, 18 Motijheel, Dacca 2
Hornsby, N.S.W.: Cnr. Bridge Road and Jersey Street, 2077
Ibadan: P.O. Box 62
Johannesburg: P.O. Box 23134, Joubert Park
Karachi: Karachi Chambers, McLeod Road, Karachi 2
Lahore: 22 Falettis' Hotel, Egerton Road
Madras: 2/18 Mount Road, Madras 2
Manila: P.O. Box 157, Quezon City, D-502
Mexico: Serapio Rendon 125, Mexico 4, D.F.
Nairobi: P.O. Box 30583
New Delhi: 4/21-22B Asaf Ali Road, New Delhi 1
Ontario, 2330 Midland Avenue, Agincourt
Singapore: 248C-6 Orchard Road, Singapore 9
Tokyo: C.P.O. Box 1728, Tokyo 100-91
Wellington: P.O. Box 1467, Wellington